Discovering

Christ's

Church

From the Bible and Those Taught by the Apostles

Bill Gothmann

 Poimen Press

To my wife, Myrna.

Discovering Christ's Church
Library of Congress Control Number: 2002090119
ISBN: 0-9717919-0-2

Poimen Press
P.O. Box 141651
Spokane, WA 99206
email: poimenpress.com

Printed in the United States of America

IN PRAISE OF LOVE

Let him who has love in Christ keep the commandments of Christ. Who can describe the [blessed] bond of the love of God? What man is able to tell the excellence of its beauty, as it ought to be told? The height to which love exalts is unspeakable. Love unites us to God. Love covers a multitude of sins. Love beareth all things, is long-suffering in all things. There is nothing base, nothing arrogant in love. Love admits of no schisms: love gives rise to no seditions: love does all things in harmony. By love have all the elect of God been made perfect; without love nothing is well-pleasing to God. In love has the Lord taken us to Himself. On account of the love He bore us, Jesus Christ our Lord gave His blood for us by the will of God; His flesh for our flesh, and His soul for our souls.

Clement of Rome, *Epistle to the Corinthians,* Chapter 49
Clement, a *"fellow worker"*, with Paul, PHIL. 4:3, wrote this at about the same time that John wrote the Book of Revelation. Clement died shortly thereafter.

TABLE OF CONTENTS

PREFACE

PURPOSE OF THIS BOOK

The Church is a most precious possession of Christ. It is His Body and His ambassador to the world. He thought so much of the church that He gave His very life for it. Oh, how He loves His Church!! The purpose of this book is to help us grow closer to this most precious possession of Christ and, in so doing, closer to the Master Himself. New Christians can benefit by cutting through the confusion of modern theological theories to the simple, direct plan that Christ gave for His Church. Church leaders from every denomination can benefit by learning what the actual pattern was for Christ's church, and guiding their congregation to the pattern Christ laid down for His Church in the New Testament. The underlying assumption is that His Church — the one in the New Testament — is the church to which we should aspire, for it is that church for which He died.

Today, Christ's church is not the same church He formed on the day of Pentecost — it has devolved. Instead of the united church presented in the New Testament, we have become fragmented by various views that have crept in throughout the centuries. We have divided into a plethora of denominations, each with a "my church" point of view, rather than a "His Church" point of view. This parochial, rather than universal, view colors everything we do, weakening His Church and making us less effective servants of Him.

In order to return to the "His Church" view, we must determine what His Church is, where it resides, what He wants for His Church and what part we play in it. The good news is that we can learn this vital information. Our first and most important source of information about His Church is, of course, the Word of God. Here, we may find the origin, His plan, and His doctrine for His Church in His words.

When we wish to learn more about a doctrine or passage, we can look further, by examining the writings of those whom the apostles taught, finding out how they believed and practiced the Word. In so doing, we will grow to believe that there were none of the divisions we have today — they all believed the same thing!! These martyrs were united in their views, presenting a greatly unified church to the world.

THE METHOD USED BY THIS BOOK

In this book, we shall examine the church of the first century: its nature, its organization, its members, its meetings, and its beliefs. The final two chapters present methods by which we can apply what we have discussed to both the Church as an organization and to our individual lives.

As we discuss each of these topics, we will first examine Bible record. Next, we shall examine comments by the early writers. I have tried to present the full range of views of early writers, especially those writing prior to 200 AD, rather than trying to skew their comments. Where there are many writings, I have given preference to the earlier writings. In some cases, little was written about a particular topic, so there are few citations.

CREDITS TO AUTHORS

The sources for this study include the Bible itself and writings of the early Christians. Most of these writings can be found in the 10-volume series, *The Ante-Nicene Fathers,* (Wm. B. Eerdsmans Publishing Company, Grand Rapids, MI), 1989. These include writings prior to the Council of Nicea in 325 AD. In addition to this hard copy series, an electronic edition is available for searching them. It is published by: Roberts, Alexander and Donaldson, James, *Ante-Nicene Fathers:* (Oak Harbor, WA: Logos Research Systems, Inc.) 1997. All Bible quotes are from *The New American Standard Bible*, (La Habra, California: The Lockman Foundation) 1977.

ACKNOWLEDGEMENTS

I wish to thank my wife, Myrna, for her careful review of the finished manuscript and her steadfast support of my writing. She has always been there when I wanted to spread my wings.

Many thanks, also, to my great Christian friend, Dave Dummitt, who critically reviewed the manuscript and made numerous, valuable contributions to its improvement.

Bill Gothmann
Feb. 6, 2002

Chapter 1

GETTING TO KNOW CHRIST'S CHURCH

INTRODUCTION

All Christians have an intense desire to know Christ better, to grow closer to Him, so they can be the kinds of people He wants us to be. It is in Him that we find our direction for life, our happiness, and our salvation. But how can we know Him better? One way is to study the Body of Christ, His Church. By studying His Body more, we can know more about what He expects of us and what we can do to please Him

But how do we get to know His Church? There are two resources that we have available to us: (a) His Word, which is our primary guide, and (b) what the early church writers — those taught by the apostles and those whom they taught — said about His Word. This gives us clues as to how to apply His Word. In this chapter, we shall examine how to study these two great resources.

GOD'S WORD

This book assumes that the Bible is God's Word and that, through His Word, we can find out the truth about His will. The Apostle Paul gives us a key understanding about God's Word when he writes, *"All Scripture is inspired by God and profitable for teaching, for reproof, for correction, for training in righteousness."* 2 TIM. 3:16. Here, the word for "scripture" is the Greek word, graphē (γραφή). We get the English words graph, telegraph, and photograph from this word. Its literal meaning is "that which is written." However, when a Jew uses it to describe a writing from God, we translate the word as "scripture," for it implies a very special writing.

The phrase "inspired of God" is translated from a single Greek word, theopneustos (θεόπνευστος). The "theo" means "God" and the "pneustos" means "breath", or "spirit." Thus, the meaning of this word is "God-breathed." That is, God breathed the sacred writings — not man.

This differs significantly from any other writing. I have written other books, but these were not God-breathed, these were Gothmann-breathed. See the difference? The Bible is a very special book and we need to acknowledge its Godly origin. It is because of this Godly origin that we can find out about the Author. Through His sacred writings we can come to know Him and His purpose for our lives.

However, notice that the writings themselves were God-breathed, not any interpretation that we may give to these writings. When we study His word, we should be very careful to correctly gather what God said, the context within which it was said, and the meaning of that writing for our lives. We should not try to read into it anything that was not there. We should always keep in mind that it is the writings themselves — the words laid down on the page — that are the inspired words of God.

STUDYING GOD'S WORD

Since we belong to Christ, we must look into His word, the Bible, to find His plan for us and for the Church. Here, we find three models of guidance that we can use to direct our paths when we read the Bible.

The first model we have are <u>commands</u> that are given to us. These are "orders" that He has specifically provided to us in His word. For example, in the Sermon on the Mount, He directs us, *"But I say to you, love your enemies, and pray for those who persecute you."* MATT. 5:44. This is an "order" directly from our Lord. Since He is Lord, we have no option but to follow it to the letter. I am bound by it and you should be bound by it.

Polycarp, a student of John's, acknowledged that we need to obey the commands of his mentors (the apostles), the prophets, and of Christ, *"Let us then serve Him in fear, and with all reverence, even as He Himself has commanded us, and as the apostles who preached the Gospel unto us, and the prophets who proclaimed beforehand the coming of the Lord [have alike taught us]."* [1]

Commands require very little judgment on our part, producing clear, black and white issues. Thus, they are the most concrete.

The second model for guidance in studying the Bible consists of <u>examples</u> that are presented in His Word. To illustrate, the early church chose elders to lead the church. *"And when they had appointed elders for them in every church, having prayed with fasting, they commended them to the Lord in whom they had believed."* ACTS 14:23. This passage, and others, provides an example to us concerning how each of the local churches were governed. Therefore, we, too, should choose elders to lead the church. Can you think of any reason we should not follow this example?

Clement, Paul's buddy, puts forth Paul as an example of patience to us, *"After preaching both in the east and west, he gained the illustrious reputation due to his faith, having taught righteousness to the whole world, and come to the extreme limit of the west, and suffered martyrdom under the prefects. Thus was he removed from the world, and went into the holy place, having proved himself a striking example of patience."* [2]

There may be occasions when some judgment might be required in using an example, as to whether we should follow it as given in the Bible. For example, Jesus rode on a donkey into

---

[1] Polycarp, *Epistle to the Philippians,* Ch. 6
[2] Clement, *Epistle to the Corinthians,* Ch. 5

Jerusalem. I doubt that He wants us to ride donkeys on our way to meetings of the Church today. However, if the example is relevant (and this may require judgment), we should try to follow these examples and we should be bound by them.

Examples require more judgment than commands. We need to assure ourselves that the examples are relevant to our present day situation. Thus, they are less concrete than commands.

The third model we have are <u>inferences</u>. Here, we infer something from a doctrine or event within the Bible. For example, Ephesus was a large church, whereas Crete was a very small church. In 1 Timothy, chapter 3, Paul writes to Timothy in Ephesus, telling him about the qualifications for deacons and elders. In Titus, Chapter 1, Paul writes to Titus in Crete and mentions the qualifications for elders, but fails to mention deacons. From these two cases, we may infer that smaller churches had few or no deacons, whereas larger churches had many deacons. You may, however, disagree with my inference because you see no connection between the size of the city and the number of deacons. That is your Christian freedom. I cannot and should not bind an inference on you when you do not see and agree with the connection. However, if both you and I see the inference, we should both be bound to practice what the inference suggests.

Theophilus (170 AD). was converted to Christ through his study of the Bible. Later, he succeeded Ignatius in Antioch — where Paul was ordained — and was one of the first Bible commentators. He uses an excellent example of inference, *"For, in like manner, as any person, when he sees a ship on the sea rigged and in sail, and making for the harbor, will no doubt infer that there is a pilot in her who is steering her; so we must perceive that God is the governor [pilot] of the whole universe."* [3]

---

[3] *Theophilus to Autolycus*, Ch. 5

Inferences require, by far, the most judgment. First, we must analyze to see if there is a connection between an event in the New Testament and our practice.   Then, if there is a connection, we need to assure that the connection is relevant to our practice today. Thus, inferences are the least concrete of the three ways of determining God's will from the Bible. However, even though they may require the most judgment, we are still under the obligation to examine them carefully and determine whether to apply them to our lives.

In summary, we have three models for determining how we should respond to the Bible: command, example, and inference.   Command is the most concrete, and inference is the least   concrete.   Command requires the least judgment, and inference requires the most judgment.

THE ROLE OF POST-APOSTOLIC WRITERS

Christ's plan was that His word be passed on to others, who would continue to propagate His Church.   Thus, Paul taught Clement of Rome and John taught Ignatius and Polycarp. Ignatius then became an elder at Antioch and Polycarp an elder at Smyrna.   These second generation saints wrote down their thoughts about Christ's Church and we can read their thoughts today about the organization, the mission, and the doctrine of the Church at that time.

In my studies of their writings over the last thirty years, I have come to understand that their honest, unspoiled views of what the Bible says provide a valuable window into what we should believe and practice.   Certainly, their writings do not have the same authority as those of God's inspired word. However, they can answer such questions as:

1.   What did Paul mean when he wrote about such things as qualifications of elders and miraculous gifts?

2.   How did Christians actually practice such things as baptism, the Lord's Supper, and music?

3.   What did the early Christians do during their worship services and when did they meet?

Their views were not colored by seminaries, denominational beliefs, or our present day societal norms. Because of this, these men were held in high honor and their writings were widely read in all of the early churches. Members were anxious to hear what friends of Paul and students of Peter and John had to say. Unfortunately, today, many Protestants have grown up to believe that everything after the apostolic age was influenced by the Roman Catholic Church. This is simply not the case. The centralization of the Roman Catholic Church took place very gradually, over a period of 500 years.

Perhaps the greatest lesson we can learn from these martyrs is how united they were in spirit and in faith. There was no Catholic Church or Protestant Church — just Christ's Church. They were united in their belief about who Christ was, what baptism was, what the focus of the Lord's Day meeting should be, and the doctrinal view of abortion. Where there were differences, each Christian accepted the other as a fellow saint, as having the same Father. Such unity won the world for Him. Can we learn this same lesson, today?

You now have the opportunity to meet these great Christians through their writings. Read what they had to say. See how their writings reinforce what God's Word says. See how they actually practiced, *"One Lord, one faith, one baptism, one God and Father of all who is over all and through all and in all,"* EPH. 4:5-6. See how many doctrines of today DID NOT EXIST in their time, and compare your beliefs to theirs.

The following paragraphs present some of these great authors. Others are given in a table at the end of this section.

CLEMENT OF ROME (30-100AD)

There was someone who knew Paul personally and wrote a letter that we can all read today. His name is Clement and Paul refers to him, *"together with Clement also, and the rest of my fellow workers, whose names are in the book of life."* PHIL. 4:3. Thus, we know that, about 61 AD, [4] Clement was at Philippi. Later, he, Linus, and Cletus were elders at Rome. While there, in about 95 AD, he wrote a fairly extensive letter to the Corinthian Church. Note that this was one year prior to the writing of the book of Revelation by John. The Corinthian church had dismissed their elders, and Clement lovingly wrote this letter, criticized them for this, and asking that they repent from this sin. Clement died soon after writing this letter. We refer to him as Clement of Rome to distinguish him from another great early Christian writer, Clement of Alexandria.

IGNATIUS (30-107 AD)

Ignatius and Polycarp were both disciples of the Apostle John. Ignatius was born about the time of Christ's death, and was, therefore, a contemporary with Paul We know very little about his life. A bishop at Antioch, he was imprisoned during Emperor Trajan's reign for his profession of Christ. He was then taken by escort on a route that, eventually, took him to Rome, where, in 107 AD, he was martyred by wild beasts for his beliefs. Along his trip to Rome, he wrote seven letters which have been preserved today. These were written to: (1) the Church at Smyrna, (2) his friend, Polycarp, (3) the Church at Ephesus, (4) The Church at Magnesia, (5) the Church at Philadelphia, (6) the Church at Tralles, and (7) the Church at

---

[4] These and subsequent dates should be considered approximate. They are best estimates.

Rome. This great man of God, this great martyr for Christ, had much to say that we can use in our lives, today.

POLYCARP (65-155 AD)

As with Ignatius, Polycarp was a disciple of John, the Apostle. He was a bishop at Smyrna, one of the seven churches mentioned in Revelation. We have his letter to the Philippians, written about 110 AD. This was a reply to a letter the Philippians had written him, requesting that (a) he give them words of encouragement, (b) Polycarp forward a letter of theirs to the Syrian church, and (c) Polycarp send to the Philippians any letters from Ignatius that he might have. It is obvious from Polycarp's letter that he knew his friend, Ignatius, was in Roman custody, but was unaware of whether he had been executed or not. Polycarp was eventually martyred in about 155 AD by being burned at the stake in Smyrna. Before he died, he was asked to renounce Christ. *"Polycarp declared, 'Eighty and six years have I served Him, and He never did me any injury: how then can I blaspheme my King and my Saviour?'"* [5]

EPISTLE OF BARNABUS (70-79 AD)

This was an extensive letter written to convince Jews that their Old Testament Messiah was Jesus Christ. In it, the author makes extensive use of the Old Testament sacrifices as an arch-type of Christ. Origen and Clement of Alexander claim that it was written by Barnabus; however the author makes no such claim. The great value of the letter is that it was written so early in New Testament history — between about AD 70 and AD 79. It was read extensively by the early church, which valued the teachings within it.

---

[5] *Martyrdom of Polycarp*, Ch. 9

DIDACHE (120 AD)

Also called the "Teachings of the Twelve," — a pseudonym[6] — this early document is a church manual, telling us what went on in the early church. It discusses such things as fasting, baptism, the Lord's supper, who is to be considered a prophet, and what events were celebrated on the Lord's day. As such, it is an extremely valuable resource for determining what the early church believed and practiced. It dates from approximately AD 120.

SHEPHERD OF HERMAS (140-160 AD)

This is a large book consisting of five "visions", twelve "commandments," and six "parables." It is highly allegorical. The Shepherd communicates truths to Hermas through these visions, commandments, and parables. It was a very popular book in the early church and carries a fairly early date of about 140-160 AD. Because of its size and its scope, it is a valuable witness to the meanings of some of the scriptures by the early Christians.

JUSTIN MARTYR (114-165 AD)

Justin was a Gentile, born in Flavia, Neaopolis, Samaria. He later traveled to Ephesus, where he encountered a Jew named Trypho, and wrote his *Dialogues with Trypho, A Jew,* presenting why Jesus is the Christ. He appears to have been well educated, eventually settling down in Rome. While there, he wrote two large "apologies" — defenses of Christianity — one to the Roman Senate and one to Emperor Antoninus. He was martyred during the reign of Marcus Aurielius in 165 AD. Thus, he is called Justin Martyr.

---

[6] They were not actually written by the twelve apostles.

OTHER WRITINGS

The above paragraphs give you a flavor for what is available in the writings of these early writers. The earliest writings will give the best clues as to what the early church believed and practiced. After all, these are closest in time to the source. The following is a list of the earliest church writings, plus some later writings that I consider interesting:

PARTIAL LIST OF EARLY CHRISTIAN AUTHORS

Author	*Date*[7]	*Description*
The New Testament	45-96 AD	Various apostolic authors
Clement of Rome	95 AD	Letter to the Corinthians asking that they repent for dismissing their elders
Epistle of Barnabus	70-79 AD	General epistle to convince Jews that Jesus was the Christ
Ignatius	106 AD	Seven epistles of encouragement to different churches while he was on the way to be executed
Polycarp	110 AD	An encouraging letter to the Philippians
Didache	120 AD	Handbook of church practices
Shepherd of Hermas	140 AD	Large letter detailing his visions, commandments, and parables
Justin Martyr	150 AD	Defends Christianity to emperor, Roman Senate, and Trypho, a Jew

---

[7] Dates are best approximation

Author	*Date*	*Description*
Tatian	150-170 AD	Defense of Christianity to the Greeks; harmony of the Gospels which we do not have
Minucius Felix	166-198 AD	Heathen-Christian argument
Theophilus	170 AD	Letter to the idolater, Autolycus
Revelation of Peter	175-200 AD	Spurious visions of Peter
Athenagoras	177 AD	Defends Christians to the Emperor
Irenaeus	185 AD	Defense against agnosticism
Clement of Alexandria	200 AD	Wrote extensive defenses of Christianity; instructs us in Christian living
Tertullian	207 AD	Prolific North African, Latin writer defending Christianity, preaching against heretics, and on Christian virtues
Hippolytus	220 AD	Refutation of philosophers
Commodianus	240 AD	Instructions for Christians against the gods of the heathens
Origen	240 AD	Prolific Christian writer and teacher; wrote a large systematic theology, a huge treatise against Celcius (a heretic), and others
Cyprian	250 AD	Correspondence of a pastor; works on Christian virtues
Eusebius Pamphilus	340 AD	Wrote noted book on church history

Author	Date	Description
Apostolic Constitutions	350 AD	Extensive handbook of church practices
St. Patrick	460 AD	Wrote of his life converting Ireland to Christ

DETERMINING PRACTICE AND BELIEF OF THE EARLY CHURCH

In each chapter of this book, we shall examine, first, what is said by the Bible. Next, if there are early church writings that give us other clues, we shall quote directly from them. In this manner, we can examine what the early church believed and practiced. We shall place the date of the writing beside the name in order to use as a guide. Keep in mind that these dates are approximate.

Chapter 2

NATURE OF CHRIST'S CHURCH

INTRODUCTION

Before we can examine the workings the church, we must first examine the most basic nature of the church. In this chapter, we shall ask four questions that lead to an understanding of that nature: (1) Who or what is the church? (2) To whom does the church belong? (3) When and how was the church born? (4) What is the mission of the church? Our understanding of what Christ wants for His Church depends upon the answers to these four questions.

WHO OR WHAT IS THE CHURCH?

We can find the answer to this inquiry by examining what the Bible says about the meaning of the word. Since the New Testament was originally written in the Greek language, we should look at what the Greek Bible says and try to determine the precise definition of the church. In the Bible, the word for "church" is the Greek word, ekklesia, (ἐκκλησία). The "ek" part of the word means "out" and the "klesia" part of the word uses the same word as our English word "call."[8] Thus, the word "church" means "called out ones." Although it is the word used extensively in the New Testament for the church, the word itself is from general Greek conversation. The Bible illustrates this in that this same word is used of the "assembly" (actually it was almost a mob) that assembled when the silversmiths were being put out of business by Paul's teachings: *"So then, some were shouting one thing and some another, for*

---

[8] Klesis (κλῆσις) is the noun form of the Greek verb, kaleo (καλέω). We get our English word "call" from this Greek verb.

the assembly was in confusion, and the majority did not know for what cause they had come together." ACTS 19:32.   In this case, ekklesia was the word used to specify a group of people meeting together for a specific purpose.

Note that "ekklesia" means a group of people. It does not stand for a building or a club, or anything else. In the first few centuries, it was only used to represent a group of people. Thus, when we say we are going to the Church, today, we are not using the word as the apostles intended; we are distorting the word. When Christ speaks of His Church, he is speaking of a group of people dedicated to Him. Our goal in life should be to be a part of this group of people that He has claimed for His own.

TO WHOM DOES THE CHURCH BELONG?

The central idea of the church is that it is Christ's Church. According to His Word, He, and only He, owns it. That is, He, and only He, owns us personally and owns the group to which we belong — His Church. The Bible tells us this in very clear language: *"And I also say to you that you are Peter, and upon this rock I will build My church; and the gates of Hades shall not overpower it."* MATT. 16:18. Note that He uses the term, "My Church." Jesus is here claiming us and the group of His people as His.

But what makes us His? What makes the group of called-out-ones His? We find the answer in Acts, where Paul instructs the Ephesian elders to guard God's church: *"Be on guard for yourselves and for all the flock, among which the Holy Spirit has made you overseers, to shepherd the church of God which He purchased with His own blood."*   ACTS 20:28. Thus, He bought and paid for us. He bought and paid for the called-out-ones. He bought and paid for all the people on this earth. With His miraculous grace, He blessed all of us by tearing down the walls between us and the Father, making us a part of His body.

Furthermore, the price He paid was one that no other person in the universe could have paid. He paid His own precious, perfect blood for us and for His Church. My life, your life, all of us on this earth were purchased with the precious blood of Christ. There is no way I could outbid that price; there is no way I would want to outbid that price. It is too high. I can't even fathom a price that great.

Thus, He paid the greatest price any one in the universe could pay for His Church. I didn't pay the price. You didn't pay the price. Only He stepped forward — only He was qualified to step forward to pay the price. And now the clincher. Wouldn't it be the height of arrogance for me to claim "His Church" as "My Church?" Wouldn't I be making the greatest mistake of my life to claim that I, along with my fellow Christians, somehow own the Church, when He, in fact He and only He, paid for it? I could not possibly think of usurping this kind of authority, of insulting my Savior by claiming the church to be My Church. Yet, we do this all the time in today's society. We have hardened our hearts for so long that it is almost considered weird to speak of His Church. Our conversation is dotted with "your church" and "my church" and "my friend's church."

Recently, I did a search of the Bible and of all the writers listed in the volumes, *Anti-Nicene Fathers,* (a ten volume set of Christian documents written prior to the Council of Nicea in 325 AD), searching for the phrases, "our church,", "my church," and "His Church." There is NO CASE in which any writer referred to "my church" (referring to himself) or to "our church." The first use of the term, "to church," meaning "to worship services" is not used until 200 AD.[9] In every case, only Christ claimed the expression, "My Church." Thus, in stark contrast to our customs today, the terms "our church" or "my church" were not used by anyone in the Church for at least

---

[9] Clement of Alexander, in *The Instructor,* Book 3, Ch. 11.

300 years. We have deviated from the pattern of the early church by moving in on Christ's claim for His Church, and I believe that it has taken a toll on His Church.

Note that, initially, we may use the term, "my church" to express the fact that this is the group of which I am a part — not that I own the church. However, using "my church" permits our minds to gradually creep from "my church" to "our church" and, finally, into the thinking process that it is a social organization owned by and governed by all of us Christians. The apostolic and post-apostolic writers were smarter than this. They recognized up front that the church is Christ's, and their language continually reflected that fact. We need to emulate their piety and their respect for Christ.

My Church Must Meet My Needs

By not using language that acknowledges Him as Head of the church and as Purchaser of the church, we put the focus on ourselves rather than on Him. If I claim it as "My Church," I expect the church to satisfy my needs. I expect it to conform to my expectations and my wishes. And, if it does not, I shall go to another church that WILL meet my needs. I will keep searching until I find a church that will meet my concept of what my church should be. I know there's one out there. I'll just keep looking until I find it.

Not only this, but, if I claim it as my church, each of us can claim a different church. Thus, no longer is there only one church — His Church — but, as we see today, there are many designer churches to satisfy every whim of man. There are churches that focus on family needs. There are churches that concentrate on social reforms. There are churches that focus on liturgy. There are churches that focus on upbeat music. There are today churches of every color to meet the needs of every person who wants his or her own church. We acknowledge this fact in the way we use the terms. You have "your church" and I have "my church." In using these terms, we are admitting that there are all kinds of churches over the globe. In this way, we are able to differentiate between churches, and I can feel smug in knowing that my church is the right church.

His Church Enables Us

I suggest that it is part of God's plan for our happiness and success that we acknowledge His Church. This plan allows us to focus on the central person of the church, Christ, rather than focusing upon ourselves. My church wants to satisfy my needs. His Church wants to satisfy Him. My church wants a pleasing worship experience for me. His Church wants only to worship Him and acknowledge Him as my Lord. My church wants to enable me to serve in a way that is pleasing to men and to me. His Church enables me to focus on serving Him and let church politics, status, and my own ego fade into the background. My church depends upon the power of me. His Church enables the power of Him through me.

Furthermore, when it is His Church, we will be insistent upon following the pattern He has established for His Church: its government, its meetings, and its salvation. My church wants to establish the typical American top down authority chain to govern it. His Church places Him at the helm and examines the Bible to determine the pattern He has established for governing His Church. My church plans meetings to meet my needs and to meet the needs of visitors. His Church meets to accomplish what He has laid out for us. My church provides salvation on my terms — a feel good approach. His Church depends upon His grace under the plan He outlines in the Bible. My church will lead me into paths that lead to my own destruction. His Church will lead me to His eternal salvation and to Him as its Author. Thus, using His plan for my life, I am enabled to become the man, the spiritual person, that God wants me to be. Using His plan for His Church, the church itself is enabled to become the body of adoring saints that He wants it to be.

The Results

The effects of viewing the church as "His Church" are mind-boggling. No longer do we focus on what we can accomplish by ourselves, but now we enable God to work His power in us as we do His will. No longer are we self-sufficient, now we are God sufficient. Origen declares, quoting Philippians 4:14, *"But how could He [Christ] ever be the Paraclete [advocate], and the atonement, and the propitiation without the power of God, which makes an end of our weakness, flows over the souls of believers, and is administered by Jesus, who indeed is prior to it and Himself the power of God, who enables a man to say: 'I can do all things through Jesus Christ who strengtheneth me.'"* [10] Christ has the power of God and so do we. No job is to tough for us to handle, or too humble for us to enjoy. We are freed to observe the working of His will in things in our lives that we could only imagine. What a faith builder!!

The effect upon His Church is also remarkable. No longer do we have to focus on finances, programs, and leadership. Now we are freed to focus on Him and let Him lead us in His path. The yoke of leadership is lifted from our shoulders as we lay our burdens at His feet, seeking His help and guidance for His Church. The Holy Spirit is freed to work in every individual, causing the church to blossom like a Texas spring day. His rainbow of energy fills everyone in the Church as they experience life-changing growth in their lives. The results are truly exhilarating for all members.

This, in turn, attracts others who want this "living water" in their lives, who want to experience the success and the joy of serving Him. Thus, church growth naturally occurs

---

[10] Origen, *Commentary on the Gospel of John*, Book 1, Ch. 38

— in accordance with His plans, guided by Him. Instead of depending upon our own church growth programs, plans, and aspirations, we yield these to Him, whose power is unleashed in the lives of all who seek Him.

By adopting the "His Church" approach, we also are an agent for unifying His Church. St. Patrick (c. 460 A.D) illustrated the humble submission that each of us need as part of His Church. *"So now I commend my soul to my faithful God, for whom I am an ambassador in all my wretchedness; but God accepteth no person, and chose me for this office — to be, although among His least, one of His ministers"*[11] He fully accepted the Lordship of God over him and the church. As a result, he was able to do what no one else was able to do — to win the people of Ireland to Christ. This was before the Roman Catholic Church, before Protestantism. His simple faith allowed him to convert a whole country to Christ. He states, *"When I baptized so many thousands of people, ..."*[12]

In this same country where St. Patrick served God by converting thousands to Him, Protestants and Catholics are now at each other's throats. Instead of unity, there is the ultimate in disunity; there is hate and intolerance. Instead of His Church, there is the Catholic Church and the Protestant Church. It has become a battle over "your church" versus "my church." If only Ireland would return to the unifying faith of their patron saint, St. Patrick. For His Church is a unifying church. His Church is a loving church. His Church leads all of us to Him — the Master who loved us so much He gave His life for us. His Church causes all who love Christ to love each other.

His Church can unify us, too, as we serve him in our local congregation. He can bring us together so that we work in harmony toward the goals He sets before us. And for us, what a joy to serve Him in His Church! Can there be any more worthy

---

[11] *The Confession of St. Patrick*
[12] Op cit

goal for all Christians than placing Him in His proper place in His Church and unleashing His power in our individual lives and in His Church?

THE BIRTH OF CHRIST'S CHURCH

The circumstances under which Christ's Church came into existence are revealed to us in Acts chapter two, where it reads, *"And when the day of Pentecost had come, they were all together in one place."* ACTS 2:1 Thus, the specific day of the birth of the church was the "day of Pentecost".   Pentecost (pente means "5") always occurred 50 days after the Passover. Jesus was crucified on Friday, the day before Passover, a Saturday. Fifty days after Passover would be seven weeks and one day. That would be a Sunday. Thus, the Church was born on a Sunday, the Day of Pentecost.

"And there appeared to them tongues as of fire distributing themselves, and they rested on each one of them. And they were all filled with the Holy Spirit and began to speak with other tongues, as the Spirit was giving them utterance." ACTS 2:2-5. Great things were happening on this day! God was showing His power and giving everyone present a "heads up." He was ushering in a new era for man and God.

Once God had their attention, then Peter preached a great, evangelistic sermon, finishing with the line, *"Therefore let all the house of Israel know for certain that God has made Him both Lord and Christ—this Jesus whom you crucified."* ACTS 2:36. Peter didn't mince words; he came right to the point. It was decision time for the listeners.

"Now when they heard this, they were pierced to the heart, and said to Peter and the rest of the apostles, "Brethren, what shall we do?" ACTS 2:37. Those who were listening recognized that they needed to respond, and they were seeking from Peter and the rest of the apostles a way to make things right with God, since they had crucified His Son.

Peter responded directly, *"Repent, and let each of you be baptized in the name of Jesus Christ for the forgiveness of your sins; and you shall receive the gift of the Holy Spirit."* ACTS 2:38.   There was nothing complicated about this. Peter asked them to repent and be baptized for the forgiveness of their sins. That would heal the wound between them and God.

What was their response? They did what Peter had asked them to do. *"So then, those who had received his word were baptized; and there were added that day about three thousand souls."* ACTS 2:41. There were no questions, no great theological discussions, no purple baptismal robes, no documents to sign, just simple men changing their lives to heal the God-man rift. Don't you thrill when you read of the simple acceptance of God's plan?

The scripture notes that *"there were added that day 3000 souls."* Who added them? Since it was Christ's Church, Christ added them. They didn't have to sign a doctrinal statement or submit to a board of inquiry, they were simply added to the church. Thus, Christ's Church was started on the Day of Pentecost, at Jerusalem, by the addition of the initial 3000 souls to His Church.

Contrast this simple beginning with today's plethora of churches. When was the Adventist Church founded? When was the Methodist Church founded? When was the Pentecostal Church founded? Christ's Church was founded at Jerusalem on the Day of Pentecost. It's that simple.

THE MISSION OF CHRIST'S CHURCH

In any organization, one of the most important questions we need to ask is, "Why are we here?" In other words, "What is our mission?" Is His Church merely an adoration society, where we adore Him, or is there more to the task? Since we are His Church, we have to look to Him to find the answer to this question. He is our Lord. He is the Head. He is our Leader. Sure enough, we find that Our Faithful Lord has set down

instructions for His Church in His Word.   In Matthew He tells
us, *"All authority has been given to Me in heaven and on earth.
Go therefore and make disciples of all the nations, baptizing
them in the name of the Father and the Son and the Holy Spirit,
teaching them to observe all that I commanded you; and lo, I
am with you always, even to the end of the age."* MATT. 28:18-20.
This scripture forms the basis for our understanding of His
mission for His Church.

This verse starts out with Christ's authority.   There are
three terms used in the Greek to express authority or power in
the New Testament. The first of these is ergon (ἔργον). This is
power that has been placed into motion, producing work. The
last part of our English word, energy, comes from this word, en
+ ergy (Greek: energia, ἐνέργια). The second of these is
dunamis (δύναμις). This is the capability of doing work. The
work has not yet been set into action. We get our words,
dynamite and dynamo, from this word.   These have the
capability of doing work. The final word used in the New
Testament for power is the word that is used in Matt. 28:18, the
Greek word, exousia (ἐξουσία), meaning the authority or power
to act. Thus, Christ has authority to act in any circumstances.
That is, He has the authority given Him as God to permeate His
Church as we go about winning new converts to Him. He has
the power to command, to love and to soften anyone's heart to
His message.

The next word in this verse is the word "therefore."
Because of His authority, because of the power He works
through us, we can accomplish His mission. We cannot do it
ourselves; we need Him. He is the great Cause of action within
us that allows us to accomplish His purpose. We have only to
yield to Him as Lord and allow His power to permeate our
existence, to flood over us like a great cloudburst of water.

Next in the verse, we are told to go. Note that we are
not to sit on our haunches and wait for others to come to us, but

we are to go. Actually, the participle, "going" is used here, and can be interpreted that we are to make disciples "as we are going."[13] As we work our daily life, those with whom we come in contact will know He is in us. We can, therefore, go to them with His message.

After the "go," there are three verbal forms within the scripture: make-disciples[14], baptizing, and teaching. However, the first is an active verb and the next two are both participles that expand on this active verb. Thus, the "baptizing" and the "teaching" tell us how to "make-disciples." As a result of this construct, we should interpret that, in this scripture, making disciples consists of baptizing and teaching. I could use a similar expression for washing my car: Go, wash my car, rinsing and drying it. The rinsing and the drying are there to indicate how to wash it. In a similar manner, the baptizing and teaching are there to tell us how to make disciples.

Although we will make more extensive comments concerning this in the chapter dealing with salvation, we should note that this verse is extensively quoted by the early writers. In the longer version of the Epistle of Ignatius (106 AD) to the Philadelphians, he quotes this verse in showing that there is a difference between the Old Testament and the New Testament.[15] Tertullian (207 AD) also quotes the verse in his discussion of baptism: *"For the law of baptizing has been imposed, and the formula prescribed: 'Go,' He saith, 'teach the nations, baptizing them into the name of the Father, and of the Son, and of the Holy Spirit.'"*[16] He asserts that baptism is a new law, part of the new dispensation.

---

[13] A participle is a word having the characteristics of both a verb and an adjective. In the present tense, this can be done by adding "ing" to a verb. For example, a baptizing person, or a teaching person.

[14] In this verse, the word disciple is used as a verb. Thus, we are to disciple people. The word "make" is not in the text.

[15] Ignatius, *Epistle to the Philadelphians,* longer version, Ch. 9

[16] Tertullian, *On Baptism,* chapter 13

Thus, the mission of His Church is to make disciples, both baptizing them and teaching them. This sounds like an entirely evangelistic mission statement. Are we ONLY to make disciples? What about ourselves and our Christian life? Ignatius (106 AD), in his Epistle to the Ephesians, understood that being a disciple was a life-long process. It was not an end, but a journey. He states, *"I do not issue orders to you, as if I were some great person. For though I am bound for the name [of Christ], I am not yet perfect in Jesus Christ. For now I begin to be a disciple, and I speak to you as fellow-disciples with me. For it was needful for me to have been stirred up by you in faith, exhortation, patience, and long-suffering."*[17] Thus, we are to continue the learning process, becoming more effective in our Christian life as we journey. We are to grow in God day by day. He and other Christians did not view being a disciple as an end, but a process. Keep in mind that the definition of a disciple is a learner, and adherer to someone else. Thus, we are to learn more about God each day and adhere more and more to those principles He has in mind for us.

SUMMARY

Who or what is the church? The church is that body of believers of whom Christ is head. To whom does the church belong? It belongs to Christ, for He purchased it with His own blood. When and where was the church born? It was born in Jerusalem on the day of Pentecost in about 30 AD. What is the mission of His Church? It is to win others to Him and to grow in our knowledge and devotion to Him. By placing Him first in our lives and in His Church, we can become both more effective disciplers of others and more effective disciples of Him who bought us.

---

[17] Ignatius, *Epistle to the Ephesians,* Chapter 3.

Chapter 3

MEMBERS OF CHRIST'S CHURCH

INTRODUCTION

In this chapter, we shall examine the membership of the church. We shall first examine how we become members, and then will examine four of the names we are given in the New Testament: members, brothers, saints, and priests. Each of these prescribes a role in which we serve. It is interesting to note that Clement (95 AD), also, refers to us in these same four terms.[18]

BECOMING A MEMBER[19]

What was the prerequisite for becoming a member? We see this in Acts 2. Peter had just preached a great sermon to the Jews who had gathered from around the world for Pentecost, trying to convince them that they had crucified the Son of God, the Messiah. As a result, the Word says they were *"pierced to the heart."* But was that good enough? No. They had to act on what they had heard. They asked of Peter and the rest of the apostles, *"'Brethren, what shall we do?' And Peter said to them, 'Repent, and let each of you be baptized in the name of Jesus Christ for the forgiveness of your sins; and you shall receive the gift of the Holy Spirit.'"* ACTS 2:37-38. Thus, first they had to repent. That means they had to literally turn their mind around (that is what "repent" means in the Greek). Instead of serving the priests, they now had to serve Christ.

The second requirement was that they had to be baptized for their sins — to wash away their sins. After all, if they just

---

[18] Clement of Rome, *Epistle to the Corinthians,* Ch. 17, 35, 40, and 46
[19] Chapter 9, *The Salvation of Christ's Church*, discusses this in greater detail.

repent, who will atone for the sins of the past? Who will pay for these? Christ will, if they obey Him in Christian baptism. For further reading on baptism, see Chapter Nine, "The Salvation of Christ's Church."

Thus, we conclude from this discussion that a willing candidate for membership in His Church is a repentant, baptized sinner. However, once one becomes a candidate for Christ's Church, how does one become a member? We see the answer in Acts, chapter 2, also. *"So then, those who had received his word were baptized; and there were added that day about three thousand souls. ... And the Lord was adding to their number day by day those who were being saved."* ACTS 2:41, 47. Who signed them up? It was Christ Himself who added them to the church. They didn't have to pass a test. They didn't have to subscribe to a set of doctrinal rules. They did not need the permission of the elders. They did not need the permission of the other members. No earthly person could add them to Christ's Church, no matter how hard he tried. Only Jesus can add us to the church. This is His exclusive role. This is as it should be, for it is His Church, not our church. He determines who is a part of it — not us.

BEING A MEMBER

It is significant that the term "member" is not used of those who were Godly in the Old Testament. It is a New Testament term. In the Old Testament, the Jews were part of a hierarchical scheme, where God was at the top, then the high priest, then priests, then elders, and, finally, individuals. The individuals had the law and the priest to tell them what to do and when to do it.

In the New Testament, The Holy Spirit is in each of us, working His will as God directs us. Thus, in the New Testament, we have been brought into the full membership of God and His Church. We each report to God directly through His Son. We are members of His Body, instead of passive observers. We are sons of Him. *"For you are all sons of God through faith in Christ Jesus."* GAL. 3:26. Wow! What a privilege!

Paul has an extended discourse on members in 1 Cor. 12:12-30. He notes first that there is unity in the Body of Christ. *"For even as the body is one and yet has many members, and all the members of the body, though they are many, are one body, so also is Christ."* 1 COR. 12:12. This unity suggests that members have a unity of (a) purpose, (b) gifts, and (c) one Head.

This last summer, my wife and I went camping in our travel trailer. While trying to make some connections to the trailer, I raised up and ran my head into the sharp corner of an open window. My immediate reaction was to go to my knees in pain and hold my hand over my bleeding skull. All of this was an immediate reaction — I didn't even have to think about it. Why did every member of my body come to the aid of my hurting head? It was because the body is united in purpose. If one part of it hurts, every part of the body comes to its aid. This same reaction should occur in Christ's body. When part of it is injured, the entire body should rush to the aid of that part. When one part is happy, all parts should share in that happiness. This is unity of purpose.

We also have a unity of gifts; the gift of the Holy Spirit is in each of us. Although the *extent* of the Gift in you and me is the same, the *operation* of the Gift is not the same. For example, while I was holding my hurting head, my right hand was held tightly over the wound while my knees were on the ground, holding me in a stable position. Thus, both of these members were equally important — my right hand for stemming the bleeding, and my knees enabling me to maintain a kneeling position. This is the same as it is in His Church. One may be a speaker, another a singer, another an encourager, another a prayer warrior. Each of us is imbued equally with the gift of the Holy Spirit at baptism, but the operation of the Holy Spirit differs in how He works within us. This unity of *extent* of His Gift but varied *operation* of His Gift permits the body to function as one for our Head, Jesus Christ.

As a body, we all report to one head. When I was kneeling, holding my hurting head, I pulled my hand away and saw considerable blood. I knew that I should seek the help of my wife to determine how serious the wound was and to dress the wound. I then got up and walked around to the door of the trailer, where she greeted me. The wound was not serious.

Notice that the head did the analysis of the situation and determined which way to go. The hand did not say, "But I think we should stay here. I can stem the bleeding." The foot did not say, "The hand is all wet. I know the direction we should go." Both the hand and the foot recognized the head as the leader. There was never a question of whom to obey.

We, too, need to seek and carry out the directions of our Head, Christ. When He provides us His leadership in His Word, we should not say, "but that is not reasonable. I think we should do this, instead." Our function should be to obey His commands, the examples He placed in His Word, and the inferences to which we are led. Our function is to place our body, His member, under His leadership, and let Him direct our lives through the Holy Spirit that He has placed within us. No longer are we our head, He is the Head. He is our Arch-Bishop, our First Overseer

This membership also has implications in the organization of the Church. Since the Holy Spirit is in all of us, we are directed individually by Him, and not through an earthly priest. If this is true, what is the purpose of the elders? They are not to serve as priests — intercessors — between Christ and us. They are to serve as organizers, as our trainers, and as our pastors, so that we can each be more effective. They are there *"for the equipping of the saints for the work of service, to the building up of the body of Christ."* EPH. 4:12. Thus, they are to equip and to oversee the process to assure that Christ's church grows in numbers and in spirit.

The membership model suggests that most decision-making should be done with the active participation of the members. The equalizing force of the Holy Spirit in all of us suggests that all contribute to the Church. The Holy Spirit does not reside solely in the elders or the deacons. Thus, the efforts of the elders should be to move decision making out to the members, and reserve, for themselves, those decisions that contribute to order and discipline.

We have examples of this model in the New Testament. In Acts 6, where the deacons were chosen, the Apostles stated the problem, turned selection over to the congregation, and then ratified the congregation's decision.

In Acts 15, Paul traveled to Jerusalem to consult about the conversion of the Gentiles. The Jewish church at Jerusalem believed that these Gentiles should be circumcised and be held to the standards of the Old Testament. Paul felt otherwise, that these Gentiles should be freed from Old Testament standards.

This was a very sensitive issue, one that could have torn the infant church apart. Thus, Paul was sent by the Gentile church at Antioch to the apostles and elders at Jerusalem. Note that Paul's home church knew what was going on — they sent him to Jerusalem.

Paul then reported to Jerusalem, where he was greeted by the entire church. Then, the elders and apostles came together to consider the problem. Note that, at this point, the members were not involved. These apostles and elders then hashed things out and came out with a solution, which they presented to the entire Jerusalem Church. They did not keep this a secret, but sought the underwriting of the members. Furthermore, the entire church decided to send a delegation to Antioch. *"Then it seemed good to the apostles and the elders, with the whole church, to choose men from among them to send to Antioch with Paul and Barnabas."* ACTS 15:22. Note that the members were actively involved.

But the process did not stop here. Paul and his delegation reported back to the Antioch Church, *"So, when they were sent away, they went down to Antioch; and having gathered the congregation together, they delivered the letter."* ACTS 15:30. Again, the members were involved.

Thus, we have, in the Bible these two models for decision making. Routine decisions should be turned over to the congregation after giving them instructions. Those of a more serious nature should be made by the elders, but the church should be informed of the problem and the decisions that were made. The elders should make every effort to involve members in the decision making process, thereby recognizing that the Holy Spirit moves in all of us.

In many of today's churches, such a problem would have been resolved between ministers. Since it was a sensitive issue, these two ministers would have met in secret and attempted, in secret, to smooth things over without involving either the elders or the congregation. In so doing, they would be hindering the Holy Spirit that is in the elders and that is in each of us. We need to remember that we are all members of Christ's Church in equal portion and that the Holy Spirit works through all of us.

We need to observe that the elders have the authority to make decisions within the congregation. As members, we need to submit to their authority. *"Obey your leaders, and submit to them; for they keep watch over your souls, as those who will give an account. Let them do this with joy and not with grief, for this would be unprofitable for you."* HEB. 13:17. God gives them this authority and we need to respect it. When the Corinthian Church dismissed their elders, Clement of Rome (95 AD) admonished them, *"Ye therefore, who laid the foundation of this sedition, submit yourselves to the presbyters, and receive correction so as to repent, bending the knees of your hearts."*[20] Thus, as members of Christ's Church, we should all submit to them as shepherds of our lives.

BEING A BROTHER

The members of the Church are also called brothers and sisters. When Jesus was told his earthly brothers were outside, He replied, *"My mother and My brothers are these who hear the word of God and do it."* LUKE 8:21. In using this term, He was declaring that we all have the same Father. Thus, we are all equal in His sight. Since we have the same Father, we are subject to the same rules, the same love, and the same organization. This means that I cannot tell another brother what is right, I can merely point out what the Father says is right. I cannot make judgments as to whether he is or is not a brother — only the Father has this right. In addition, because we both have the same Father, I would not want to incur the Father's wrath by insulting or mistreating one of the Father's offspring.

This colors our entire life. Because we know that Jesus died for each person, we must treat each with the respect and dignity that our Father would want. We can not, for example, be a part of racial discrimination. Rather, we are to be the peacemakers that enable all of us to live in peace. When I am speaking to a class of students, I must treat each with the respect that a son of God is due. Whatever I do, wherever I go, I am obligated to My Father to treat all of His Children with the respect that He would want.

Being a brother also means that I can go to my Christian brothers when I am in need. One summer, I found myself commuting from Spokane, Washington to the Pullman-Moscow area for school at Washington State University and the University of Idaho. My first class was at 7:30 AM, so I had to

---

[20] Clement of Rome, *Epistle to the Corinthians*, Ch. 57

get up at 4AM to make the 80 mile, 2 hour commute. However, as the semester wore on, I found that I was running short on time. I could not keep up with the home work and the commute. I had a minister friend, Dewey Obenchain, who lived in Colfax, a town about 14 miles from Pullman. I then called him and asked if I could stay at his place for two nights of the week to ease my time constraints. "No problem," he said. "You can stay in my travel trailer." This eased the problem and I was able to finish the semester. In fact, Dewey felt free to ask me to teach a class at the Church he served. Brotherhood works two ways!

You can treat brothers this way. You can call them up and ask if you can stay at their house. They are there for your help and assistance when you need them. I believe that we are too polite, as Christians. We *call* others brothers, but we *treat* them the same way we treat people at work. This should not be. The early church was so close that they took their meals together. We need to develop that closeness to each other that comes by genuinely knowing and loving members of the family. We need to learn to depend upon one another.

BEING A SAINT

The Greek word used for saint is the adjective, hagios (ἅγιος).[21] Its fundamental meaning to the Greeks was "one who was set aside — was consecrated — for a religious purpose." It also inferred purity. In the Bible, it is usually translated "saints" or "holy ones," reflecting that those within Christ's Church were set aside, consecrated, to the work of Christ. Note that it was applied to all Christians, because all were considered dedicated servants of King Jesus. Paul very frequently used the term, saint, to refer to the Christians in a particular community. For example, *"to all who are beloved of God in Rome, called as saints."* ROM. 1:7. The term is used 61

---

[21] Greeks frequently wrote just the adjective, leaving out the noun.

times in the New Testament, and every time it refers to ALL the Christians at a particular place.   Thus, ALL Christians are rightly called saints.

Being a saint has its privileges and its obligations. We have the privilege of working side by side with Jesus Christ in His Church. He could have set up His Church in such a manner that we would only be spectators, but this was not His will. He allows us to be full participants.   What a privilege, to be associated with the God of the universe.

It also has its obligations. It means that I am something special. I am set aside for Him. I cannot live as those in the world, but I must live as a servant of Christ. This means that I will seek righteousness in all that I do, rather than seeking a way around righteousness. I am not seeking the short-cut; I am seeking the right cut.

This also means that I do things for His sake, not merely because I want to or like to do them. It means that my goals in life conform to His purpose for me. It means that I seek His will in everything I do. I am His servant and wish to serve Him. Each of us relishes being used by Him for His purpose, for in Him we find our greatest joy and our greatest purpose.

BEING A PRIEST

We are also called priests in the New Testament. John says, *"and He has made us to be a kingdom, priests to His God and Father; to Him be the glory and the dominion forever and ever."* REV. 1:6. As such, we are not ordinary folk. We are set aside to worship Him. As Christians, we have the obligation to our High Priest to keep ourselves pure so that we can serve Him.

A priest offers incense; we offer prayers. A priest eats the holy bread; we eat the communion bread. A priest offers up sacrifices for sin; Jesus is our sacrifice.   A priest teaches what God commands; we teach His Holy Word.   A priest celebrates holy days; we celebrate the Lord's Day as our holy day. A priest sacrifices weekly; we come to the Lord's table to remember God's sacrifice weekly. A priest knows God's word; we should know God's holy word. A priest serves under a high priest; we serve under our High Priest, Jesus. Only a priest is permitted to enter the Holy Place; we are permitted direct access to God the Father through Jesus Christ. Thus, there are many ways in which we are priests.

There is one more important aspect of a priest. He is a participator, not a spectator. A priest cannot serve his high priest by being idle. We cannot serve our High Priest by sitting idly by and watching others serve. To be a priest, we have to be actively serving Him.

Unfortunately, many churches today are relegating their members to the spectator role. Instead of active participation, they seek a passive role for their members. All singing is done by a professional choir and all speaking is done by a professional speaker. Some have gone so far as to relegate the Lord's Supper to a minor role, preventing their members from sharing in this vital, participative role. In contrast to this, His Church is active. His Church provides opportunity for all to participate fully in the Priesthood of Christ.

Chapter 4

ORGANIZATION OF CHRIST'S CHURCH

INTRODUCTION

The foundation of Christ's church is the members, with Christ as it's head. However, did Christ have a more detailed plan for the organization, or did He leave this up to chance or up to us? If He did have a plan, have we followed it? Where can we find His plan? In this chapter, we shall look at what Christ wants for the organization of His Church.

THE NAME OF CHRIST'S CHURCH

First, let us next examine what Christ named His Church. Is it named after a man? Is it named after a doctrine? Is it named after a place? To get the answer to this question, we can look into our text, the Bible. An examination of the scriptures shows that the following names were used for the church:

Name Used	Times Used
Church or churches (without any modifier)	81
Church or churches of God	12
Church or churches of or in a place (Ephesus, for example)	8
Churches of Christ	1
Church of the first born	1
Churches of the saints	1

I should explain that Hebrews 12:23 refers to the Church of the first born, those who entered prior to the coming of Christ, and those who were the initial recipients of the Gospel when Christ came. Thus, this is the church that has within it the first born. The term, churches of the saints, is used in 1 Corinthians, where Paul states, *"for God is not a God of confusion but of peace, as in all the churches of the saints."* 1 COR. 14:33. The term, "saints," simply means holy. Thus, this is the church of the *holy ones*. To be holy is to be set aside for a spiritual use. Therefore, this refers to us: members of His Church who have been set aside to Him. These last two phrases thus refer to the collective members of His Church. Note that they do NOT refer to an individual member.

The volumes of the *Ante-Nicene Fathers* use the words, "church" or "churches" 3646 times. As in the Bible, most of the time the terms are used without a modifier. There is frequent use of geographical places for modifiers — the Church at Ephesus, for example. The terms "Church of God" and "Church of Christ" are used very frequently. The only time a term is used for a person is "churches Irenmus" — a heretical church. There is also a smattering of such terms as holy catholic (meaning universal) church, triumphant church, apostolic church, and Christian Church. Thus, it would seem that the early church stuck very closely to the Biblical use of names for His Church.

From this analysis, it is apparent that, when referring to the universal church, these writers referred to it as "the church" or attached a Godly term to it, such as "Church of God" or "Church of Christ." If they had to differentiate between individual congregations, they did this by naming the place where the individual group resided: Ephesus, Corinth, or Philippi, for example.

The church was never named after a particular human being. There is no Pauline church, Johnnine Church, or James' Church, for example. In fact, Paul derided the Corinthian church for such divisions in Christ's Church: *"Now I mean this, that each one of you is saying, 'I am of Paul,' and 'I of Apollos,' and 'I of Cephas,' and 'I of Christ.' Has Christ been divided? Paul was not crucified for you, was he? Or were you baptized in the name of Paul? I thank God that I baptized none of you except Crispus and Gaius, that no man should say you were baptized in my name."* 1 COR. 1:12-15. Paul would be very upset if a church were to be named, "St. Paul's Church." We, as followers of Christ, should not name His Church after any human being: Paul, Apollos, Cephas, Luther, Tyndale, or any of the great men of God.

The universal church was never named after a doctrine. There is no Lord's Supper Church, Salvation Church, Preaching Church, or Baptism Church, for example. His Church is named after God, after a place, or after the body of saints attending there. Is there any reason we should not follow the example given to us in the New Testament and give the name to His Church that He has shown us by example? It would be a tribute to Him if we were to follow this example.

Denominationalism

Christ's Church is one; it is united in Him as both Author of His Church, and Head of His Church. Under His plan, there is no room for splitting His Church into the many denominational factions that exist today.

I am deeply moved by the fact that Christ, on the eve of His crucifixion, prayed, not for His deliverance, but for the unity of His believers. *"And the glory which Thou hast given Me I have given to them; that they may be one, just as We are one; I in them, and Thou in Me, that they may be perfected in unity, that the world may know that Thou didst send Me, and didst love them, even as Thou didst love Me."* JOHN 17:22-23. Through all the pain and agony He was enduring, He thought of us and our unity. He states that the reason for this great desire of Him was so that the world might come to know Him. Unity was essential in order to evangelize the world.

Boy, have we let Him down! We have split His Church into so many factions that the message He had for the world is lost in the discord of voices advocating divergent doctrines and practices. His clear message of hope and salvation has been replaced with a rampant desire to soothe, entertain, and dumb down the audience concerning His Word. We have introduced so many doctrines foreign to His Word, that ferreting out His original message becomes a real trial to the reader.

We have introduced the term, "denomination," into our daily vocabulary. The "de" in this term means "away from" or "down" and the "nomination" means "to name." Thus, we have developed a zeal to "name ourselves away from" other Christians — in contrast to His prayer for unity at Gethsemane. This is apparent in how we use the word, denomination. How many times have you heard someone say, "His Denomination"? It's always, "our denomination." Denominations belong to man, not God. Why have we treated His Church with such disregard and, in so doing, ignored His earnest appeal on the eve of His death?

THE HEAD OF CHRIST'S CHURCH

Christ's Church has Him as the Head. It does not have an earthly head. Six times in God's Word, Paul states that Christ is the Head — five times, head over the church (Eph. 1:22, 4:15, 5:23, Col. 1:18, 2:19) , and one time, head over all rule and authority (Col. 2:10). I have a personal principle I use in my life. If the Bible says a thing one time, I should listen. If it says something twice, I should really perk up. Here, the Bible says it five times. It's trying to tell us something, folks. Listen up!! Christ and only He is Head of Christ's Church. The *Ante-Nicene Fathers* echo this tune. Twenty times they affirm that Christ is Head of the Church.

When we acknowledge that Christ is Head of His Church, two things happen. First, we recognize that everything we do within the church must stand the test of God's Word, since this lists our marching orders. When we wish to raise money, we look in the Word to figure out how to do it. When we wish to evangelize, we look in His Word for instructions. When we wish to select leaders, we look to The Book to determine what the qualifications should be and how to do it.

The second effect this has is to place all of us on an even playing field. We're all servants of the Head, Jesus. His Holy Spirit is in all of us and no one has a corner on the market for determining which direction to take. We are all members of His holy body. You support me and I support you. As a result, the Holy Spirit works through all His saints, and ideas are generated and options are revealed. In this manner, the best choices can be made for the church, and each of us feels he/she had a part in the process. The body, the family works as a unified unit to accomplish His will.

THE OFFICERS OF CHRIST'S CHURCH

We can look into God's word to determine what people He chooses to lead His Church. One list is given in Ephesians: *"And He gave some as apostles, and some as prophets, and some as evangelists, and some as pastors and teachers, for the equipping of the saints for the work of service, to the building up of the body of Christ"* EPH 4:11-12. It should be noted that the construction of the Greek in this sentence indicates that the pastor is also a teacher. All pastors will be teachers, but all teachers will not necessarily be pastors. Note also that this list excludes some other possible officers we find in other parts of the Bible. Phil. 1:1 addresses overseers and deacons. In Acts 14:23, Paul appoints elders. Romans 16:1 lists Phoebe as a (female) servant — in Greek, a deaconess. Thus, our possible list of officers in the church includes: apostles, evangelists, pastors, overseers, elders, teachers, deacons, and one deaconess.

Before we examine each of these, let us think about officers. Each officer should have, in the Bible, (a) a job description, (b) a list of qualifications, (c) a method of appointment, and (d) examples that we can follow in the Word. Can we find each of these in the Bible for the above list of officers? We shall examine each of these in the following paragraphs.

APOSTLES

The Greek word used in the New Testament for "apostle" is apostolos (ἀπόστολος). The "apo" part of the word means "from" and the "stolos" part means "to send." Thus, it is one sent forth. One of the best English words to describe an apostle is "ambassador." It is one sent forth to represent someone else.

The word was a common one in the Greek language. In Romans 16:7, Andronicas and Junias are called apostles; in Phil. 2:25, Epaphroditus is referred to as "your apostle;" in 2 Cor. 8:23, Paul calls some unnamed brothers, apostles (NASB uses "messenger". It is the Greek word apostolos, however).

The critical question is, however, who was appointed an ambassador for *Christ*? We understand these to be the twelve plus Paul. Matthew 10:2 lists each of the twelve, referring to them as apostles. In 1 Cor. 1:1, Paul specifically refers to himself as an apostle of Jesus Christ. Thus, these thirteen people were the Apostles of Christ.

When Judas died, the remaining apostles felt that it was necessary to replace him, and did so in Acts 1:15-26. In verses 21 and 22, Peter lists the qualifications for being an apostle: *"It is therefore necessary that of the men who have accompanied us all the time that the Lord Jesus went in and out among us— beginning with the baptism of John, until the day that He was taken up from us—one of these should become a witness with us of His resurrection."* Thus, the qualifications they set forth for becoming an apostle required that the man walk with Christ while He performed His public ministry on this earth.

The one exception to this requirement was that of Paul. On numerous times, he claims to be an apostle of Jesus Christ (Rom. 1:1, 1 Cor. 1:1, 2 Cor. 1:1, Gal. 1:1, Eph. 1:1, and others). However, he recognizes that he was chosen in a special manner, *"Then He appeared to James, then to all the apostles; and last of all, as it were to one untimely born, He appeared to me also. For I am the least of the apostles, who am not fit to be called an apostle, because I persecuted the church of God."* 1 COR. 15:7-9. Here, he admits that his was a special apostleship, outside of but equal to the appointment of the twelve.

Note that it is impossible for there to be apostles of Christ today, for there is no one alive that accompanied Jesus while He walked this earth. Thus, the apostle is not an office within His Church today.

Summary of Apostles

Office:	APOSTLE
Job Description:	One sent forth by Christ.
Qualifications:	Must have accompanied Jesus on this earth during His public ministry.
Appointment:	Directly by Christ or by the group of apostles.
Examples:	The twelve and Paul.

EVANGELISTS

The word, evangelist, is used only three times in the New Testament. In Acts 21:8, Philip is called an evangelist. In Ephesians 4:11, it is included in the list of church officers. In 2 Tim. 4:5, it is used of Timothy, where he is told to do the work of an evangelist. In addition, Irenaeus, Clement of Alexandria, Tertullian, Hippolytus, Origen, and other post-Biblical writers frequently referred to Matthew, Mark, Luke, and John as evangelists. Thus, we have abundant evidence of the existence of this office.

However, just what was this office? We get a great clue from examining the word "evangelist." In the New Testament , the Greek word for evangelist is euangelistēs (εὐαγγελιστής). The "eu" means "good" ; the "angelistēs" means "announcer." This "announcer" part of the word is the same word used for "angel": one who announces. Thus, an evangelist is one who announces the good message: the gospel. (The word for gospel has the same roots: eu + angelion — a good message). So, we must conclude that an evangelist is one who preaches the gospel: the good news of Christ. In the *Ante-Nicene Fathers*, the writers of the New Testament books are frequently called evangelists. This seems reasonable, since each of them was preaching the gospel — in this case through the written word — and this is the job of an evangelist.

If we assume that both Timothy and Titus are evangelists, we note that each of them was to appoint elders within the church. Titus is told by Paul, *"For this reason I left you in Crete, that you might set in order what remains, and appoint elders in every city as I directed you."* TIT. 1:5. Thus, the church is said to be in order when these elders are chosen.

Eusebius Pamphilus wrote an extensive book on church history in about 340 AD, An extremely capable historian, his book is with us today. In it he discusses the mission of the evangelist, *"Afterwards leaving their country, they performed the office of evangelist to those who had not heard the faith, while with a noble ambition to proclaim Christ, they also delivered to them the books of the holy gospels. After laying the foundation of the faith in foreign parts as the particular object of their mission, and after appointing others as shepherds of the flocks, and committing to these the care of those that had been recently introduced, they went again to other regions and nations, with the grace an cooperation of God."* [22]   We can conclude from these accounts that the purpose of an evangelist was to preach the gospel in a new area, appoint elders, and turn the leadership of the church over to these elders. They would then move on to establish new churches in new areas. Note that this is precisely what Paul did.   *"And when they had appointed elders for them in every church, having prayed with fasting, they commended them to the Lord in whom they had believed."* ACTS 14:23. Paul then returned to Antioch.

As to qualifications of the evangelist, 1 Timothy, 2 Timothy, and Titus provide us with some very general criteria. There is no specific list of qualifications. An evangelist can be either married or unmarried. An evangelist can be young or old. They are to fight the good fight, to prescribe and teach, and to use their spiritual gifts. Paul charges Timothy, *"That you keep the commandment without stain or reproach."* 1 TIM. 6:14.

How were evangelists appointed?   Paul directly appointed both Titus and Timothy. The Apostles appointed Philip as (apparently) a deacon and an evangelist. In addition, Paul advises Timothy, *"Do not neglect the spiritual gift within you, which was bestowed upon you through prophetic utterance with the laying on of hands by the presbytery."* 1 TIM. 4:14. Thus, he was commissioned by the elders. Note that the deacons in Acts 6:6, were also set aside by the laying on of hands of the apostles.

Do we have evangelists today?   I believe we do. Anyone who feels called by the Lord to preach the Good News can be set aside by the local elders for this work. Their mission would then be to win others to Christ, establish a new church, appoint elders within that church, and turn the leadership over to the elders of that new church. They would then be free to repeat the process.

---

[22] Eusebius Pamphilus, *Ecclesiastical History,* Book 3, Ch. 37

We have, however, departed from the pattern of His Church we see in the New Testament. Instead of an evangelist, we usually seek out a "pastor/minister/preacher/reverend" to start a new church, and then have the "pastor/minister/preacher-/reverend" lead that church until he feels led to go to another church. Instead of accepting Paul's challenge to Titus of "setting the church in order," we assume it is in order when the "pastor/minister/preacher/reverend" is selected. This is NOT the New Testament pattern for His Church. We shall comment on this more extensively in the chapter, *"Ministers of Christ's Church"*.

Summary of Evangelists

Ministry:	EVANGELIST
Job Description:	Preach the good news, start churches, appoint elders, then move on.
Qualifications:	Quite general.
Appointment:	Appointed by elders, apostles or Christ
Examples:	Timothy, Titus, Philip

Chapter 5

ELDERS OF CHRIST'S CHURCH

INTRODUCTION

Because of its importance, we will spend this and the next chapter discussing the office of elder (or pastor) in Christ's church. In this chapter, we will examine the office itself: What is it? And what do these people do? As we will find, the modern church has greatly confused this most important office. In the next chapter, we shall examine the qualifications of this office and the selection process used by the early church.

DEFINING PASTORS, OVERSEERS, AND ELDERS

The Bible uses three terms to describe pastors: pastors, overseers, and elders. These three offices are, in fact, the same offices. The key verses are in Acts: *"And from Miletus he sent to Ephesus and called to him the elders of the church. ... Be on guard for yourselves and for all the flock, among which the Holy Spirit has made you overseers, to shepherd the church of God which He purchased with His own blood."* ACTS 20:17, 28. We first note that these were elders. Second, we note that they are to shepherd (the word for pastor), the flock. Third, they are called overseers. Thus, all three names are used to refer to the same group of men.

We can identify their job description a bit closer by examining these three words. First, they are to be shepherds. The English word, pastor, occurs only in Eph 4:11 with the list of possible church officers. The Greek word that is used for both pastor and shepherd throughout the New Testament is poimēn (ποιμήν), a derivative of the word for flock (poimnē ποίμνη). Thus, a pastor or shepherd is one who cares for a flock — feeds it, protects it, and helps it grow.

The second word applied to the Ephesian elders is "overseer."   Here, the Greek word used is episkopos (ἐπίσκοπος). The "epi" means "over" and the "skopos" means "to look." We get the word, scope, from "skopos". Thus, an episkopos is one who oversees.   This same word was transliterated into Old English as "bisceop," and, from the there, arrived in modern English as "bishop." As can be seen, the word, bishop, is the same word as episkopos. Note that the original meaning of "bishop" was identical to the meaning of the word "overseer."   Therefore, an elder was an overseer, a bishop, a pastor, and a shepherd.   These terms were synonymous in the early church.   Only later did the terms bishop and elder diverge.

The word, overseer, was a common word in Greek. It was used of a person who took care of a Greek secret society — kept the books, paid the bills, and, in general, acted as caretaker of the society.

The third word used for this group of men is "elder." In English, we use the terms old, older, and oldest. In Greek, the terms are, presbus, presbuteros, and presbutatos,[23] where elder is presbuteros — older. The Greek meanings are identical to those in English. Thus, an elder is an older person — not old, not oldest, but older. In many of the early writings, the word "presbytery" is used to refer to the group of elders; the words, "elders" and "presbytery" are interchangeable. The English word "Presbyterian" also comes from the Greek term, to denote that this particular church uses elders. In addition, the English word "presbyopia" derives from the same Greek word; this is the condition of having "older eyes", eyes needing glasses because of aging of the eyes. The English word "priest" also has its derivation in the word presbyter.

Peter further defines who the elder should be when he admonishes the elder about his attitude, "... *nor yet as lording it*

---

[23] Greek: πρεσβυσ, πρεσβυτεροσ, πρεσβυτατοσ

over those allotted to your charge, but proving to be examples to the flock. And when the Chief Shepherd appears, you will receive the unfading crown of glory" 1 PETER 5:2-4. They are not to lord. That is, they are not to act as lords and others as servants to them. They are to lead by example.

There is a word in Greek word, archē (ἀρχή), which means "first" in the sense of being the beginning. We get the prefix, arch- from it, as in arch-enemy, arch-duke, archive, or arch-bishop. In the New Testament, it is quite often used of rulers, as in Luke 12:11 where we are not to be anxious when we are brought before rulers; also, in Titus 3:1 where we are told to be subject to our rulers. I believe it is significant that it is NEVER used of the elders. They are never to be first-rulers. It is, however, used in the 1 Peter passage above, where Christ is called the chief-shepherd (literally, the arch-shepherd). Thus, the arch-bishop of all elders is to be Christ Himself: they report directly to Him. The elders are not to be first-rulers, nor are they to report to any man who is first-ruler. Again, many churches have departed from Christ's church by appointing men to be arch-bishops, when Peter himself told us that Christ has that title.

We now have a pretty good idea of who this group of men are. They are to be older, they are to shepherd and care for the flock, and they are to oversee the affairs of the church without lording it over them.

NUMBER OF ELDERS

In the Bible, the number of elders is always greater than one. There is never a case when an elder (or a bishop) leads a church. Rather, it is a group, a team operation. The following are examples:

1. Acts 14:23: Paul appoints elders in the churches
2. Acts 15:2, 4, 6, 15, 22, 23: Paul consults the elders of the Jerusalem church
3. Acts 20:17, 28: Paul speaks to the Ephesian elders

4. Acts 21:18: Paul visits the Jerusalem elders again
5. Phil. 1:1: Paul addresses his epistle to the church and the elders
6. 1 Tim. 5:17: "Let the elders who serve well be worthy of double honor."
7. Titus 1:5: Titus directed by Paul to appoint elders in every city
8. James 5:14: If we are sick, we are to call for the elders of the church
9. 1 Peter 5:1: Peter exhorts the "elders among you."
10. Rev. 4:4, 10, and others: 24 elders praise God

Polycarp (110 AD), also, in his letter to the Philippians acknowledges multiple elders, both in the saints that are with him and in the Philippian church, *"Polycarp, and the presbyters with him, to the Church of God sojourning at Philippi;"*[24] *"Wherefore, it is needful to abstain from all these things, being subject to the presbyters and deacons, as unto God and Christ."*[25] Clement (95 AD), a friend of Paul (see Phil. 4:3) assumes multiple elders as he writes in his letter to the Corinthians, *"being obedient to those who had the rule over you, and giving all fitting honor to the presbyters among you."*[26] The Shepherd of Hermas (140 AD) also refers to multiple elders, *"But you will read the words in this city, along with the presbyters who preside over the Church."* [27] Thus, the earliest of the post-apostolic church writers acknowledge multiple elders.

There NEVER is a case of a church in the New Testament with one elder, one pastor, one bishop, or one overseer (since these are all the same people). This is God's

---

[24] *Epistle of Polycarp to the Philippians,* salutation
[25] *Epistle of Polycarp to the Philippians,* Chapter 5
[26] *First Epistle of Clement to the Corinthians,* Chapter 1
[27] *Shepherd of Hermas,* Second Vision, Ch. 4

plan for His Church. Note that we violate this constantly in today's society. It is very common to have one pastor of a church — in direct contrast to the many examples we are given in the New Testament. Again, we have departed from God's Church and are creating our own church.

Very shortly after the close of the New Testament, parts of the church started elevating one elder above the rest and calling only him a bishop. The first evidence of this is in the writings of Ignatius, who was martyred in 107 AD. He writes to the Ephesians, *"Wherefore it is fitting that ye should run together in accordance with the will of your bishop, which thing also ye do. For your justly renowned presbytery, worthy of God, is fitted as exactly to the bishop as the strings are to the harp."* [28] Clement, writing about 95 AD, and Polycarp, writing about 110 AD, and Shepherd of Hermas (140 AD) all believed in a single level of eldership, whereas Ignatius, writing about 107 AD, believed in multiple levels. Within 11 years of the close of the New Testament, parts of the church had begun to deviate from God's plan for His Church as shown in the New Testament.

A HUMAN HEAD OF THE CHURCH?

After the apostolic era, the levels of church officers continued to increase, until, finally, one was considered at the top and claimed to be the top official of the church — in stark contrast to the humble elders who served His Church in the New Testament. Peter, it is claimed, was the first earthly head of the Church. However, Peter never claimed that title. In 1 Peter 1:1 he identifies himself as an apostle — not a super-apostle. Note that Paul wasn't bashful about proclaiming himself an apostle. In Ephesians 1:1 and in many other passages he identifies himself as an apostle. Finally, Jesus was not bashful about the extent of His authority. He asserts, *"All*

---

[28] Ignatius, *Epistle to the Ephesians*, Chapter 4

authority has been given to Me in heaven and on earth." MATT. 28:18. Why was Peter bashful about claiming to head the earthly church, if he was?

Some claim that Christ gave papal authority to Peter in Matthew, *"And I also say to you that you are Peter, and upon this rock I will build My church; and the gates of Hades shall not overpower it."* MATT. 16:18. However, let us examine the Greek. In it, Christ says, "you are Peter". The word used for Peter is Petros (Πέτρος). It is in the masculine case, for it refers to a man. It is also a common Greek word for a stone that one might hold in his hand, and was used in "Homer and the Illiad" for the stone that a warrior threw.

The verse then proceeds, "upon this rock." (Greek: epi tautē tē petra, ἐπὶ ταύτῃ τῇ πέτρᾳ). The epi (ἐπὶ) means "on", the tautē (ταύτῃ) is a feminine pronoun meaning "this very" — demonstrating that it was this very rock. The tē (τῇ) is a feminine article most easily translated as "the". In Greek, the pronoun (tautē), article (tē), and the noun (petra) all have to agree in gender. Thus, if the noun is feminine, the pronoun and the article are made to be feminine.

Finally, there is the word petra (πέτρα). It is a feminine word, meaning a large, land-mass of rock; the Rock of Gibraltar would be an example. Thus, the phrase, "this rock" could not have referred to Peter. First, there is a difference between petros, a stone, and petra, a large rock mass. Second, Peter is masculine and "this rock" is feminine. It would have been the same as saying, "He is Peter and upon her (referring to Peter) I will build my church." That does not make sense.

Then to what does "this rock" refer? I suggest that it refers to Peter's confession, *"Thou art the Christ, the Son of the living God,"* in the previous verse. It is upon this rock that the entire church is based. If He is not the Son, then the whole church crumbles. On the other hand, if He is the Son, then this forms the basis for His Church.

I should note that Origen (240 AD) believes that "this rock" refers to every Christian. All are part of the rock of Christ. *"For all bear the surname of "rock" who are the imitators of Christ, that is, of the spiritual rock which followed those who are being saved."* [29] He notes further that John 20:22-23 gives the same power to the rest of the disciples that He gave to Peter.

Let us now examine the purported line of succession of heads of the church (popes). Linus, Cletus, and Clement of Rome are purported to be the second through fourth popes. These three were all presbyters in Rome at the same time. Note that there is not a hint in Clement's letter to the Ephesians (95 AD) about any of the three being head of the church. In fact, none of the three are mentioned at all. Their names are also absent from such early documents as Epistle of Barnabus (75 AD), and the generally accepted versions of Ignatius (106 AD). Ignatius was quite bishop centric. If anyone would have mentioned them, he would have. Their names are also absent from Polycarp's letter (110 AD), the Didache (120 AD), the Shepherd of Hermas (140 AD), Justin Martyr (150 AD), Tatian (160 AD), Minucius Felix (170 AD), Theophilus (170 AD, although he mentions a Greek named Linus, the teacher of Hercules), and Athenagoras (177 AD).

Irenaeus (185 AD) is the first to write that there was a succession of bishops at Rome: Linus, Cletus, and then Clement. He also names Polycarp as bishop of Asia, and, later in the document, seems to indicate that all churches were under the domination of the Roman church. In his books, Irenaeus is attempting to show that, unlike the heretics Valentinus and Marcion, Christian doctrine has a direct line to the apostles. To do this, he presents a succession of Roman bishops.

I would suggest, however, that this was a radical departure from the pattern in the New Testament. Christ's

---

[29] Origen, *Second book of the Commentary on Matthew,* Book 12, Ch. 11

Church was governed by local elders who acted as overseers on behalf of Christ. Thus, the only archbishop they reported to was Archbishop Jesus Christ, *"And when the Chief Shepherd appears, you will receive the unfading crown of glory."* 1 PETER 5:4. In this passage, the Greek word used for "Chief Shepherd" is archipoimēn (ἀρχιποίμην). The "archi" means "first" or "chief" and the "poimēn" means shepherd or pastor. Thus, Peter is referring to Jesus Christ as being the arch-pastor, or (since a bishop and a pastor are the same person) arch-bishop. Isn't it interesting that Peter, supposedly the first pope, refers to Jesus as his arch-bishop? After Peter refers to Jesus as an arch-bishop, wouldn't it be impossible to believe that he would ever refer to a human church official as an arch-bishop?

THE RESPONSIBILITIES OF THE ELDERS

From the title, it is apparent that the elders are to (a) be older, (b) oversee, and (c) shepherd the flock. Their age gives them a perspective that leads to great stability of the church. Proverbs declares, *"A gray head is a crown of glory; It is found in the way of righteousness."* PROV. 16:31. In the Old Testament, the word, "elders", is used 141 times. God's people, the Jews, recognized the wisdom of older men and placed them at the head of every family synagogue, and temple. When Christ established His Church, it was natural that He used the same organization that had been used for over two thousand years, placing elders at the head of the local body.

The elders in His Church are to oversee. That is, they are to supervise every phase of His Church — both spiritual and physical. They are responsible for the teaching, the preaching, the counseling, the finances, the maintenance of the physical plant, the supervision of staff, the music, the youth, the Bible School, the benevolence, and every thing else that the church needs. They can not do all this themselves; that is why they are called "overseers." Their job is to train people to do, then oversee that doing.

Note that some modern churches have changed the responsibilities of the elder. They place them ONLY over the spiritual needs of the congregation, letting the deacons take charge of the physical needs. The elders can delegate whatever they wish to deacons, but the elders are still in charge of ALL parts of the church.

The elders are also to be pastors. That is, they are responsible for all teaching, preaching, comforting, and counseling. Again, they cannot do all this themselves — they need the congregation to act as a family to assist them in their ministries. However, they bear the responsibilities for these spiritual phases of the church, not the "pastor."

We have changed this ministry, too. Many churches have placed a "pastor" in charge of the preaching, counseling, and staff. This was not the pattern His Church had in the New Testament. The elders were responsible for these phases of the church, too. Again, they can delegate, but they are still responsible. If they choose to delegate their preaching responsibility to another person, that is just fine. However, that person is responsible to the elders for what is preached.

Members of the church have been mis-trained to expect the "pastor" to do the job of the elder. They expect him to call on them, to see them when they are ill, to counsel them, to preach, and to do just about everything else the elder should be doing. It is no wonder, that such "pastors" burn out. God's plan was a pastoral oversight by all of the elders, not appointment of a Chief Executive Officer. We have "Americanized" His Plan, choosing the business model, rather that the model we see in the New Testament.

What can we do? We can educate people about what the Bible teaches — that the elders are the overseers, not "the pastor." When they are ill, they should call one of the elders. Shepherding programs can be initiated where each person within the church has his/her own elder to whom they can look for help and guidance. We can return "Our church" to "His Church."

CONCLUSION

As can be seen, both the Bible and post-apostolic writers agree that the early church was led by a plurality of elders, and that each of these had the duties of (a) overseeing, (b) pastoring, and (c) being mature, elder men. By contrast, the modern church has greatly confused the office of pastor from what it was in the early church. We have confused their definitions, the number of pastors selected in each congregation, and their responsibilities.   It is no wonder that Christians today have digressed from Christ's Plan for His Church.

Chapter 6

QUALIFICATION AND SELECTION OF ELDERS

INTRODUCTION

In order for there to be an office, there must be qualifications and a method of selection. In this chapter we shall first examine what the Bible has to say about these qualifications, and then refer to early church writers as to how these qualifications were understood. We shall then examine selection processes used within the Bible.

QUALIFICATIONS

The qualifications for the elder are laid down in specific terms in two places within the Bible: 1 Tim. 3:1-7 and Titus 1:6-9. We should note that most of these qualifications are those required for any Christian. Others are more restrictive than those for the general member. The Timothy passage reads, *"3:1 It is a trustworthy statement: if any man aspires to the office of overseer, it is a fine work he desires to do. 2 An overseer, then, must be above reproach, the husband of one wife, temperate, prudent, respectable, hospitable, able to teach, 3 not addicted to wine or pugnacious, but gentle, uncontentious, free from the love of money. 4 He must be one who manages his own household well, keeping his children under control with all dignity 5 (but if a man does not know how to manage his own household, how will he take care of the church of God?); 6 and not a new convert, lest he become conceited and fall into the condemnation incurred by the devil. 7 And he must have a good reputation with those outside the church, so that he may not fall into reproach and the snare of the devil."* 1 TIM. 3:1-7.

The Titus passage reads, *"if any man be above reproach, the husband of one wife, having children who believe, not accused of dissipation or rebellion. 7 For the overseer must be above reproach as God's steward, not self-willed, not quick-tempered, not addicted to wine, not pugnacious, not fond of sordid gain, 8 but hospitable, loving what is good, sensible, just, devout, self-controlled, 9 holding fast the faithful word which is in accordance with the teaching, that he may be able both to exhort in sound doctrine and to refute those who contradict."* TITUS 1:6-9.

In the following paragraphs, we shall describe these characteristics, taking into account the meaning of the underlying Greek words.

Desire for the office:

The first prerequisite of an elder is that he should desire the office. The word "aspire" is the Greek word oregō (ὀρέγω). It means to reach out for something. Thus, it is a desire for the office. One should also notice that this is a work. The office is not given as a reward or as an honor. Expression of desire should include actually doing the work.

Must the individual go to the leadership of the church and say, "I want it! I want it!", or should the leadership or congregation take the initiative? I suggest that, for a model, we look to Deut. 1:15 and Acts 6. In the first case, men who were already experienced tribe leaders were apparently approached by Moses to be leaders of tens, fifties, hundreds, and thousands, *"So I took the heads of your tribes, wise and experienced men, and appointed them heads over you, leaders of thousands, and of hundreds, of fifties and of tens, and officers for your tribes."* DEUT. 1:15. In the case in Acts, the leadership charged the congregation to do the selecting. The congregation then, apparently, approached the men and asked them if they would assume duties, *"But select from among you, brethren, seven men of good reputation, full of the Spirit and of wisdom, whom we may put in charge of this task"*. ACTS 6:3.   Thus, it seems to be the responsibility of the existing leaders to search out others who can lead.

Reputation

The reputation of the elder must be such that he is not open to any censure by anyone, or open to any possible public investigation. He should be a decent and orderly person. In addition, he should be a good witness to the community. [30] It is important that the community look up to these men, for it is the community that must be won to Christ. If they cannot trust the elder, they may very well not trust the leader of the elder, Jesus.

Disposition

An elder is to be sound of mind; that is, he is to be a sober-minded individual. He is not to be greedy or covetous of either money or power.   He is to love good people and good things. He is to be a fair person, one who does not insist on the letter of the law, but is considerate of those with whom he deals. He is to behave justly, fulfilling his duty toward God and toward all men. He is to be one who loves strangers.[31]

Temper

An elder must exercise self control. This self control should govern all phases of his life — his habits, his speech, and his dealings with others. He must not be quick-tempered, quick to fight, or quick to strike another person. Thus, the peace of Christ should shine through him.   He must not be

---

[30] 1 TIM. 3:2, TIT. 1:6, 1:7; 1 TIM. 3:2, 1 TIM. 3:7
[31] TIT. 1:8, 1 TIM. 3:2, TIT. 1:7, 1 TIM. 3:3, TIT. 1:8, 1 TIM. 3:3, TIT. 1:8, TIT. 1:8, 1 TIM. 3:2

dominated by self interest. If he is to pastor, he must put the well-being of the sheep above his own well-being.[32]

Ability to Teach

An elder must look on the righteous side of life, rather than on that which is unrighteous. Thus, he must reflect the righteousness of Christ. He is to hold fast onto the faithful word according to what he was taught, and be skilled at teaching others. Part of pastoring is to be a patient, skilled teacher. He is not to be a neophyte Christian. An elder must show the wisdom that comes with time and experience as a Christian.[33]

Treatment of Wine

The Timothy passage quoted above uses the term *"temperate,"* I TIM. 3:2. This comes from the Greek word, nēphō (νήφω), which is defined as, "free from the influence of alcoholic beverages." In addition to this, both the Timothy and the Titus passages quoted above use the phrase, "not addicted to wine." This phrase means, literally, "not lingering at wine." It can be interpreted as not given to wine, and carries the connotation against the brawls that wine can engender. Wine was a common drink in New Testament times.

In Romans, Paul advises, *"It is good not to eat meat or to drink wine, or to do anything by which your brother stumbles."* ROM. 14:21. In this passage, he is indicating that, to some, eating a particular meat may cause a friend to stumble. As a Jew, Paul probably had in mind fellow Jews who could not eat meats prohibited by Jewish law. He was also indicating that, for some, drinking wine can be a stumbling block. Possibly, here, he was referring to someone who was an alcoholic.

---

[32] TIT. 1:8, 1:7; 1 TIM. 3:3, TIT. 1:7, 1 TIM. 3:3, TIT. 1:7
[33] TIT. 1:8, TIT. 1:9, 1 TIM. 3:2, 1 TIM. 3:6

We take note that there are three places within the two passages that warn against excess wine: not addicted to wine (both Timothy and Titus) and temperate (Timothy). According to the Gothmann Rule, if the scripture says it once, listen up. If it says it twice, really listen up. If it says it three times, go to maximum alert. Wine can be a problem — a big problem — to the elder. Not only can it hinder his life, but it can hinder the lives of people who see him drinking.

Although he does not totally prohibit wine, Clement of Alexandria (200 AD) observes, *"I therefore admire those who have adopted an austere life, and who are fond of water, the medicine of temperance, and flee as far as possible from wine, shunning it as they would the danger of fire."* [34]

I decided many years ago that God has prepared many types of beverages for me to drink. I can select from tea, coffee, soft drinks, lemonade, fruit drinks, water, milkshakes, milk, vegetable drinks, and a host of other products. When He has provided such a great selection, why would I want to partake of a beverage that dims my mental faculties? I'm already dim enough; I don't need any more help. Commodianus, (240 AD) in addressing drunkards, seems to agree, *"Be it mine to drink of the best things and be wise in heart."* [35]

My reasoning goes like this. Now, let me see. This beverage will dim your mental faculties, can cause you to get killed if you drive, and could easily hurt your testimony as a Christian. This other one will not. Hmmm. Not a tough choice.

The scripture tells us, *"abstain from every form of evil."* 1 THESS. 5:22. The Greek word for "form" is eidos (εἶδος), from

---

[34] Clement of Alexandria, *The Instructor,* Book 2, Ch. 2
[35] Commodianus, *Instructions,* Ch. 77

which the word "idol" has its roots.[36]   Thus, we are to avoid anything that even has the appearance of evil, even if the substance is not evil.   If anything has the appearance of evil in our society today, it is this substance.   Alcohol is associated with drunk driving, the breakup of families, gambling, public drunkenness, and all other sorts of evil.   Can you think of any *good* reason that I would want to be associated with something of such foul reputation?   I cannot.   Therefore, I choose to abstain. I recommend it highly to others.

Husband of One Wife.

He is to be the husband of one wife.[37]   This term has been interpreted variously as (a) must be married but cannot be a polygamist, (b) may or may not be married, but if so, must not be a polygamist, (c) can not be divorced and remarried, and (d) can be divorced, but not be remarried.   The Bible gives us a substantial clue when Paul addresses the widows in 1 Tim. 5:9. Paul indicates that she is a widow indeed if she has been a one man woman (enos andros gunē, ἑνὸς ἀνδρὸς γυνη). Obviously, from this passage, Paul is speaking about having more than one man in her lifetime, not having more than one man at once.   He uses precisely the same language in 1 Tim. 3:2 for the elder.   He must be a one woman man (mias gunaikos andra, μιᾶς γυναικὸς ἄνδρα).   If chapter five refers to one spouse in a lifetime, it makes sense that chapter three refers to the same criterion.

Many early writers state that it was digamy that Paul opposed.   Digamy is defined as being married to more than one spouse throughout your lifetime — at once or in sequence. Thus, it includes divorce and remarriage, the death of a spouse and the marriage of the surviving spouse, and polygamy.

---

[36]   Eidos (εἶδος) can also have a good connotation.   In Luke 9:29 it is said of Christ Himself.
[37]   TIT. 1:6, 1 TIM. 3:2

Tertullian (207 AD) states, *"Thence, therefore, among us the prescript is more fully and more carefully laid down, that they who are chosen into the sacerdotal order must be men of one marriage; which rule is so rigidly observed, that I remember some removed from their office for digamy."*[38] He observes, further, *"Why, how many digamists, too, preside in your churches; insulting the apostle, of course: at all events, not blushing when these passages are read under their presidency* [this is the person who presides]*!"*[39]

Athenagoras, (177 AD), supports this position, *"'For whosoever puts away his wife,' says He, 'and marries another, commits adultery;' not permitting a man to send her away whose virginity he has brought to an end, nor to marry again. For he who deprives himself of his first wife, even though she be dead, is a cloaked adulterer, resisting the hand of God, because in the beginning God made one man and one woman, and dissolving the strictest union of flesh with flesh, formed for the intercourse of the race."* [40]

Apostolic Constitutions (350 AD) also echoes this position, *"We have already said, that a bishop, a presbyter, and a deacon, when they are constituted, must be but once married, whether their wives be alive or whether they be dead; and that it is not lawful for them, if they are unmarried when they are ordained, to be married afterwards; or if they be then married, to marry a second time, but to be content with that wife which they had when they came to ordination."* [41] Origen (240 AD), also, says, *"And as he [Paul] selects for the episcopate a man who has been once married rather than he who has twice entered the married state."*[42]

---

[38] Tertullian, *On Exhortation to Chastity,* Chapter VII.

[39] Tertullian, *On Monogamy,* Chapter XII.

[40] Athenagoras, *A Plea for the Christians,* Chapter 33.

[41] *Apostolic Constitutions,* Book 6, Chapter 17

[42] Origen, *Against Celsus*, Book 3, ch. 48

It must be admitted that some later authors suppose that Paul was speaking against bigamy or polygamy.   Let us carefully examine this argument. Would Paul have preached against polygamy to the elder, but not have said a word about it to the rest of the church members? If it were a problem within the church, he certainly would have addressed it. Yet, he is silent on the subject. Because of this, it is very difficult to believe he was addressing polygamy when he wrote concerning elders.

From the foregoing arguments, it is clear that, indeed, digamy was that to which Paul was objecting.   Many contemporary commentaries agree with this conclusion. The elder must be a person who has been married only once in his lifetime.

Modern day churches have wanted to change this. "How can God discriminate?", they ask. Yet, if we examine the Old Testament, we will find the same type of discrimination used of the priesthood: priests with physical deformities, were not permitted to serve at the Lord's altar. *"No man among the descendants of Aaron the priest, who has a defect, is to come near to offer the Lord's offerings by fire; since he has a defect, he shall not come near to offer the bread of his God."* LEV. 21:21. Thus, it is not unexpected that God would expect a special person to oversee the Priesthood of Christians. Again, it is His Church, and we should not try to make it into "our church."

The Children of the Elder

The Timothy passage reads, *"He must be one who manages his own household well, keeping his children under control with all dignity."* We first note that the elder must be one who manages his household well. He is to be the leader in that household and he is to do a good job of leadership. Paul goes on to say that if he cannot be a good leader at home, he should not be a candidate to lead the church.

Paul writes that the elder is to "have children in subjection." The Greek for the word, subjection, is the same word used in the marriage relationship, the word hupotagē, (ὑποταγη). It is a military term meaning to "rank yourself under." Thus, children are to "rank themselves under" their father. Paul then uses the phrase "with all dignity." The children are to treat their father with the dignity that the father is due.

Titus uses the phrase, *"having children who believe, not accused of dissipation or rebellion."* The children of the elder must be believers, that is, Christians. If he cannot witness successfully to those within his own home, how can he witness to those outside the home? I suggest that this sentence applies only to children within the home. Once they become adults, they are no longer subject to their father's rule.

The children of the elder should live a life in a manner that they cannot be accused of excess or riotous living, such as that which was done by the prodigal son. In addition they should not be in rebellion to the laws and rules of living of our society or of the home.

A common question about these passages is whether the elder (a) MUST have children or (b) if he has children, they must believe? The word, "have" used here means to have or hold onto. We must keep in mind why Paul is setting forth this requirement. He wants elders who are firmly committed to Christ, and who can keep an orderly home life. He also wants mature men. When a man has children who are raised as believers and who are under his proper control, this permits him to be a good pastor of other fathers who are having problems within their family.

Apostolic Constitutions (350 AD) recommends the following for a bishop, *"Such a one a bishop ought to be, who has been the 'husband of one wife,' who also has herself had no other husband, 'ruling well his own house' In this manner let examination be made when he is to receive ordination, and to be placed in his bishopric, whether he be grave, faithful, decent; whether he hath a grave and faithful wife, or has formerly had such a one; whether he hath educated his children piously, and has 'brought them up in the nurture and admonition of the Lord;'"* [43] Thus, marriage to not more than one wife was required and, in addition, he must have raised his children in Christ. Notice that the passage assumes he has children.

Summary of Qualifications:

Christ is looking for a "few good men" to lead His Church. These should be men that are devoted fathers and husbands, pure in heart and pure in life, and dedicated to Christ and His Church. These are people that can serve as examples to the rest of the flock. What a privilege it is to serve the King of Kings in this work.

THE SELECTION OF THE ELDERS

The Bible gives us only general guidance in determining how to select elders. Let us examine some examples of selection.

In Exodus 18:17-23, Jethro advised Moses to select leaders of thousands, hundreds, fiftys, and tens to judge the people so Moses would not wear out. Moses did as he suggested, *"So Moses listened to his father-in-law, and did all that he had said. And Moses chose able men out of all Israel, and made them heads over the people, leaders of thousands, of hundreds, of fifties and of tens"* EX. 18:24-25. This infers that Moses, himself, did the selecting. However, when Moses recited this again in Deuteronomy, he stated, *"So I took the heads of your tribes, wise and experienced men, and appointed*

---

[43] *Apostolic Constitutions,* Book 2, Ch. 2

them heads over you, leaders of thousands, and of hundreds, of fifties and of tens, and officers for your tribes." DEUT. 1:15. Thus, he appointed those who were already in charge — elders who already were heads of tribes. From this, we can conclude that (a) Moses had a part in the choosing and (b) the tribes had a part in the choosing.

When we examine Acts, Chapter 6, we see a similar pattern. Here, the Hellenistic widows were being neglected from food distribution. The Apostles saw the problem, and asked the congregation to solve it, *"And the twelve summoned the congregation of the disciples and said, 'It is not desirable for us to neglect the word of God in order to serve tables. But select from among you, brethren, seven men of good reputation, full of the Spirit and of wisdom, whom we may put in charge of this task. But we will devote ourselves to prayer, and to the ministry of the word.' And the statement found approval with the whole congregation; and they chose Stephen, a man full of faith and of the Holy Spirit, and Philip, Prochorus, Nicanor, Timon, Parmenas and Nicolas, a proselyte from Antioch. And these they brought before the apostles; and after praying, they laid their hands on them."* ACTS 6:2-6.

Note the order in the selection process. First, the Apostles set down the criteria for selection. Next, the congregation did the selecting. Finally, the apostles confirmed their selection. Thus, from this we conclude that both the congregation and the Apostles had an active part in the selection process.

Finally, let us examine how Paul appointed elders in Acts, chapter 14. Paul traveled from Iconium (vs. 1) to Lystra (vs. 6) and to Derbe (vs. 6). He then returned to Lystra, Iconium, and, finally, Antioch (vs. 21). Along the way he appointed elders, *"And when they had appointed elders for them in every church, having prayed with fasting, they commended them to the Lord in whom they had believed."*

ACTS 14:23. One would conclude from these verses that Paul only did the selection.

However, let us examine his route more closely. We note that in this, a two-year, missionary journey, his itinerary took him from Syrian Antioch to Salamis, Paphos, Attalia, Perga, Pisidian Antioch, Iconium, Lystra, Derbe, Lystra, Iconium, Pisidian Antioch, Perga, Attalia, and back to Syrian Antioch. His travel over the 700 miles of sea and 500 miles of land would, itself, cost him about a month. This would leave 23 months for the 13 stops listed in the text, permitting him to stay an average of 54 days in each city. How could he, in this brief time, "train elders" in every city he visited along the way?

The answer lies in the fact that "training elders" was not mentioned in the text. Rather, he "appointed elders". The Greek word used for Paul's appointing, (cheirotoneō, χειροτονέω) is one that was originally used in the Roman Senate for voting. Later, in Paul's time, it came to mean the general term for appoint. It is also used of those who were appointed by the churches in Greece to accompany Paul in carrying their gifts to the poor saints in Judea in 2 Cor. 8:19.

Titus and Timothy are not told to "train elders", either. Titus is to "appoint elders." Here, the term (kathistēmi, καθίστημι) means to "set in place", thus to appoint to a position of authority. This is the same term used in Acts 6:3 when the Apostles "appointed" the seven deacons. Clement of Rome (95 AD) uses this same Greek word three times in the following two passages where, he points out how the elders at Ephesus were chosen, *"And thus preaching through countries and cities, they* [the apostles] *appointed the first-fruits [of their labors], having first proved them by the Spirit, to be bishops and deacons of those who should afterwards believe. Nor was this any new thing, since indeed many ages before it was written concerning bishops and deacons."* [44]   *"Our apostles also*

---

[44] Clement of Rome, *First Epistle to the Corinthians,* Chapter 42

knew, through our Lord Jesus Christ, and there would be strife on account of the office of the episcopate. For this reason, therefore, inasmuch as they had obtained a perfect fore-knowledge of this, they appointed those [ministers] already mentioned, and afterwards gave instructions, that when these should fall asleep, other approved men should succeed them in their ministry. We are of opinion, therefore, that those appointed by them, or afterwards by other eminent men, with the consent of the whole Church, and who have blamelessly served the flock of Christ in a humble, peaceable, and disinterested spirit, and have for a long time possessed the good opinion of all, cannot be justly dismissed from the ministry.." [45]
Thus, we are assured that they were appointed by apostles or others and had the full consent of the church.

Considering the above evidence, I suggest that Paul appointed elders the same way Moses in Deuteronomy and the Apostles in Acts 6 made their appointments: that he selected already existing leaders of the congregations to be elders, confirmed their appointment, and set them aside (probably by the laying on of hands). This would be consistent with a Jew (and Paul was a Jew) and his upbringing. Thus, I suggest that the selection process today should have three components: (1) the individual himself, (2) the congregation, and (3a) in an existing church, the body of elders or, (3b) in a church without elders, the evangelist. How these play together should be left up to the individual congregation. Some congregations may choose to elect elders, upon approval of the existing elders. Some may choose to merely confirm those whom the elders put forth. The Bible is not precise in giving us instructions, but, apparently, both the congregation and the appointing authority must be involved.

There are some churches that are concerned that elders might be too old. Thus, they choose "younger elders." This

---

[45] Clement of Rome, *First Epistle to the Corinthians,* Chapter 44

could be because they assume elders are to be in charge of ministries. However, this is not a correct view. Elders are to oversee ministries. They do not, necessarily, need to be in charge of these ministries. Apostolic Constitutions (350 AD) provides that the elder should not be younger than fifty years old, *"But concerning bishops, we have heard from our Lord, that a pastor who is to be ordained a bishop for the churches in every parish, must be unblameable, unreprovable, free from all kinds of wickedness common among men, not under fifty years of age;"* [46] This seems, to me, to be a good guide.

However, again, some churches have deviated from the Biblical process. In some congregations, elders are elected without any input from the existing elders. In other cases, elders are chosen by existing elders without any input from the congregation. The Bible suggest that both are required. Other churches have created such offices as junior elders, elders-in-training, ruling elders, and the like, departing from the Bible's simple instructions. I recently answered the doorbell at my house and was greeted by a young man about 18 years of age, who told me he was an elder in his church. (Hmmm. That must make him a younger older — an oxymoron). He certainly was not an elder in Christ's Church. We need to return to His Church and use His plan for appointing elders within His Church.

SUMMARY OF ELDERS

Ministry:	ELDER
Job Description:	Pastor and oversee the local church
Qualifications:	Older, married with children, and other qualifications.
Appointment:	By congregation and either present elders or evangelist

---

[46] *Apostolic Constitutions*, Book 2, Ch. 1

Examples: Ephesians (Acts 20:17,
                             1 Tim. 5:17)
                             Jerusalem (Acts 15 and others)
                             Crete (Titus 1:5)
                             Revelations (In heaven)

Chapter 7

MINISTERS OF CHRIST'S CHURCH

INTRODUCTION

The title of this chapter purposefully uses the term minister. That is what a deacon, deaconess, and preacher are within the church: ministers. Deacon and deaconess come from the same Greek word: one is masculine, the other is feminine. Let us first examine the deacon (the male). The word, deacon, comes from the Greek word diakonos (διάκονος). It was originally used of a table-server, but, later, came to mean any servant. It is contrasted with the word "slave", in that "deacon" emphasizes the work of a servant, whereas "slave" emphasizes the position of the person to the master. The word is translated as servant and as minister throughout the New Testament.

DEACONS

Acts 6 contains the accepted passage for the selection of the first deacons. *"1 Now at this time while the disciples were increasing in number, a complaint arose on the part of the Hellenistic Jews against the native Hebrews, because their widows were being overlooked in the daily serving of food. 2 And the twelve summoned the congregation of the disciples and said, 'It is not desirable for us to neglect the word of God in order to serve tables. 3 But select from among you, brethren, seven men of good reputation, full of the Spirit and of wisdom, whom we may put in charge of this task. 4 But we will devote ourselves to prayer, and to the ministry of the word.' 5 And the statement found approval with the whole congregation; and they chose Stephen, a man full of faith and of the Holy Spirit, and Philip, Prochorus, Nicanor, Timon, Parmenas and Nicolas, a proselyte from Antioch. 6 And these they brought before the apostles; and after praying, they laid their hands on them."* ACTS 6:1-6. We note that the word, deacon, is not used within the passage. However, the root word for deacon is used three places: in verse 1, "serving" (diakonia, διακονία — service); in verse 2, "serve" (diakoneō, διακονέω — to serve); and in verse 4, "ministry" (diakonia, διακονία — service). For this reason, most people accept that these are deacons who were chosen.

In Philippians 1:1, Paul addresses deacons along with elders (overseers). In 1 Tim. 3, he addresses the qualifications for the deacon. Thus, it is an office recognized by Paul. The writings of the early church are replete with references to deacons, including Clement (95 AD), Ignatius (106 AD), Hyppolytus (220 AD), and many others. Irenaeus (185 AD) writes, *"And still further, Stephen, who was chosen the first deacon by the apostles... ."* [47] Thus, there is no doubt that the office of deacon was a part of the early church, and these early authors recognized Acts 6 as the initiation of that office.

THE RESPONSIBILITIES OF THE DEACONS

What were the duties of the office? In Acts, they were chosen because there was a need. The Apostles did not have enough hands to do all the work that needed to be done and the Hellenistic widows were being neglected. Thus, they were appointed to assist the Apostles in their work.

Note that, whereas the book of 1 Timothy addresses the office of deacon, the book of Titus does not. Ephesus, where Timothy was the evangelist, was a very large city. Thus, it probably was a very large church requiring a large number of hands to do the job. Crete, where Titus was the evangelist, probably had a very small church and, therefore, did not need deacons. The job, then, was to assist the leadership of the local

---

[47] Irenaeus, *Against Heresies,* Book 3, 12:10

church, in whatever needs the church had. Ignatius (106 AD) places them in subjection to the elders, *"Let the laity be subject to the deacons; the deacons to the presbyters; the presbyters to the bishop; the bishop to Christ, even as He is to the Father."* [48] (Ignatius had elevated one elder above the others and called him a bishop). Cyprian (250 AD) points out that the Apostles were appointed by Christ, whereas the deacons were appointed by the Apostles. Therefore, the deacon should respect authority.[49] From the above, it is apparent that deacons are appointed to assist the elders, and, therefore, are subject to the elders.

THE QUALIFICATIONS OF THE DEACONS

What are the qualifications for the deacon? We find these in 1 Timothy, *"Deacons likewise must be men of dignity, not double-tongued, or addicted to much wine or fond of sordid gain, but holding to the mystery of the faith with a clear conscience. And let these also first be tested; then let them serve as deacons if they are beyond reproach. Women must likewise be dignified, not malicious gossips, but temperate, faithful in all things. Let deacons be husbands of only one wife, and good managers of their children and their own households. For those who have served well as deacons obtain for themselves a high standing and great confidence in the faith that is in Christ Jesus."* 1 TIM. 3:8-13. They must be men of dignity. That is, they must be serious about their business, a sense of gravity and dignity that promotes reverence. They must speak consistently, not one way to the elders to whom they report and another way to the flock. The wording for his relationship with wine differs slightly from that of the elder. However, both are cautioned about the dangers of too much wine.

---

[48] Ignatius, *Epistle to the Smyrnaeans (longer version),* Ch. 9. There are two manuscripts of this letter in existence today; one longer in length than the other.
[49] Cyprian, *Epistle 64,* Chapt. 3

With the deacon, a testing period is desirable; no such testing period is mentioned for the elder. Since the deacon is to perform specific tasks, perhaps Paul wishes Timothy to assure that the person will be successful in those tasks before appointing him permanently. It is presumed that the elder is capable of leading, or he would not be chosen to lead. Note that both are to be "beyond reproach."

In the Greek, there is no word for "wife." The word "woman" is used. Thus, we must determine from the context whether the passage refers to a wife or a woman. In this passage, since Paul discusses deacons, then women, then deacons again, it seems reasonable to assume that he is addressing the wife of a deacon in 1 Tim 3:11. Thus, she is to be dignified, not a gossip, temperate, and faithful. It is easy to see that a good wife can be a great asset to a deacon and his ministry, but a bad wife would be a great weight on his ministry.

The same marriage restriction is used of the deacon that was used of the elder: one womaned man: (mias gunaikos andra, μιᾶς γυναικὸς ἄνδρα).   If digamy is presumed prohibited for the elder, then digamy is prohibited for the deacon.

Whereas the elder is to have believing children, the deacon must be a good manager of his children and his household. There is no requirement to have believing children. This could be because it is presumed that the elder would have older children who could believe, whereas the deacon could be a younger man, having small children.   The deacon and the elder both must also be a good managers of their households.

THE SELECTION OF THE DEACONS

The method of appointment is detailed in Acts 6. Note the order in the selection process. First, the Apostles set down the criteria for selection.   Next, the congregation did the selecting. Finally, the apostles confirmed their selection. Thus, from this we conclude that both the congregation and the Apostles had an active part in the selection process.

THE DEACONESS

Next, we need to examine the deaconess. This term is used once in the Bible, *"I commend to you our sister Phoebe, who is a servant of the church which is at Cenchrea."* ROM 16:1. The word "servant" is the feminine form of deacon, (diakonos, διάκονος). There is a problem with using this term to represent an office, however. First, there is no job description, beyond her being a servant. Second, nowhere in the Bible is it addressed as an office. Third, there are no qualifications listed for it, if it is an office. Finally, there is no mention of it as an office for at least 100 years following the apostolic age, whereas the office of deacon is well represented in early writings.

Another interpretation of the term is that a deaconess is the wife of a deacon. If this is the case, then the deaconess is addressed in 1 Tim. 3:11, when Paul speaks of women.

Apostolic Constitutions (350 AD) says the deaconess is a ministry to women, *"Ordain also a deaconess who is faithful and holy, for the ministrations towards women."* [50] Keep in mind that this document is from about 350 AD, and offices had started to proliferate. However, even at this late date, the author does not place her at the same level as the deacon, *"For these are your high priests, as the presbyters are your priests, and your present deacons instead of your Levites; as are also your readers, your singers, your porters, your deaconesses, your widows, your virgins, and your orphans: but He who is above all these is the High Priest."* [51] Note that, whereas deacons are compared to Levites, deaconesses are in the same list as readers, singers, porters, widows, virgins, and orphans. Thus, it appears that this document recognizes the deaconess, but places them

---

[50] *Apostolic Constitutions,* Book 3, Ch. 15
[51] *Apostolic Constitutions,* Book 2, Ch. 25

along side other ministries of the church. Later on in Apostolic Constitutions, a liturgy is given for ordaining a deaconess.

One post-sixth century document, claimed to be written by Ignatius (but was not), seems to indicate that, at that time, deaconesses were widows who were enrolled in the church, *"I salute the keepers of the holy gates, the deaconesses in Christ. I salute the virgins betrothed to Christ, of whom may I have joy in the Lord Jesus."* [52].

Given the above evidence, I suggest that the deaconess is a service that all women of the church can perform. Just as all of us can minister to Christians, so women can minister to Christians. However, none of the evidence supports that the deaconess is at the same official level as the deacon.

SUMMARY OF DEACONS

Ministry:	DEACON
Job Description:	Serve the local elders
Qualifications:	Man of dignity, Married with children, and other qualifications.
Appointment:	By congregation and elders
Examples:	Acts 6, appointment of the seven, Ephesian deacons, Philippian deacons

FUNCTION OF THE PRESENT-DAY MINISTER

Thus, we have concluded that the offices of the church today consist of evangelists, pastors, and deacons. Where does the present-day, full time minister fit into this program? First, we need to readily admit that there was no such position in the early church. There were only the three offices: evangelist,

---

[52] Ignatius, *Epistle to the Antiochians,* Ch. 12. This is one of the six spurious epistles of Ignatius. These claim to have been written by Ignatius, but were not. They were probably written after the sixth century.

elder, and deacon; and the elder had oversight of the whole church. Thus, the minister is a present-day phenomenon.

We can now ask the question, *"Is he an evangelist?"* The definition of an evangelist is one who preaches the gospel, starts a church, sets aside elders, then turns the reigns of leadership over to the elders. This does not fit the role of the present day minister. Instead of doing primarily evangelism, he does extensive pastoral duties. Instead of turning the leadership over to the elders, he usually either leads the church himself or he works with the elders in leading the church. Instead of moving on when elders are appointed, the church considers him an in-place leader. Thus, he does not match the role of evangelist.

Is he an elder? If he is one, he must be married and be an older man. However, it is very common to see a younger man placed as a minister. Furthermore, there is usually no requirement for the minister to be married. Thus, he is not necessarily an elder. In many churches, he leads practically every program in the church. Thus, he appears to be a super-overseer. But this violates the doctrine of having multiple, equally-powered elders. Therefore, we can only conclude that the present day minister is not an elder.

Is he a pastor? The pastors are the elders. They must satisfy the requirements to be an elder. They must be married, have believing children, and be selected by both the congregation and the elders. They must be there for the long term. Based upon these criteria, even though many churches call this guy a pastor, he is NOT a pastor.

Is he a deacon? The purpose of the deacon is to assist the elders. The elders are responsible for all ministries within the church. This includes the preaching (the minister does this), the pastoring (the minister does this), and the general operation of the church (the minister does this). Since the minister performs functions that the elder performs, we have to suppose that he has been given this responsibility by the elders, much as the elders give any deacon responsibilities. Thus, the office of deacon best fits his role. Furthermore, he, along with everyone else in the church, is subject to the elder. Thus, this fits his role, too. Finally, we call him a minister. That is precisely what a deacon is — a minister. The only difference is that he is a minister of preaching, or a minister of visitation, or whatever role the elders decide should be his.

However, the office of a deacon has specific requirements with respect to marriage: *"Let deacons be husbands of only one wife, and good managers of their children and their own households."* 1 TIM. 3:12. Thus, he must be married, whereas a modern day minister may or may not be married. Although the office of deacon most closely fits his role, we have to exclude the minister from universally being a deacon because he does not universally satisfy the qualifications listed in the New Testament to be a deacon. We are left with the terms "minister" and "preacher" to describe this guy and his role. These are excellent, descriptive terms of his activities, so why don't we just call him the minister and leave it at that?

The real question for His Church is whether ministers will subject themselves and their ministries to the plan given in the Bible. Will they reject the title, "pastor" in favor of a term that will give the real pastors their due as listed in the Bible? Will they accept their role to be in subjection to and be an extension of the elders? Will they promote His Church or try to make it their church? The answers to these questions will determine whether His Church will grow in Him or whether His Church will just be another religious organization.

Chapter 8

MEETINGS OF CHRIST'S CHURCH

INTRODUCTION

In this chapter, we shall look at two topics: when did the church meet and what did they do when they met? First, however, we need to examine some terms used by both the Bible and early writers. In Acts 2, it says, *"And they were continually devoting themselves to the apostles' teaching and to fellowship, to the breaking of bread and to prayer."* ACTS 2:42. The early church was concerned with four activities:

(a) Apostles' teaching. This was a study of both written and oral teachings passed down from the apostles.

(b) Fellowship. The Greek word here is koinōnia (κοινωνία). The best translation of this word is "sharing." It included sharing in food, as in Acts 6:2, and sharing in material wealth. It also included sharing in Spirit, as in 2 Cor. 13:14 (fellowship of the Spirit) and sharing in the work of the gospel, as in Phil. 1:5

(c) Breaking of bread. This could be interpreted as either sharing a meal or sharing the Lord's supper. However, since the word "fellowship" included sharing meals, it more probably meant to be sharing in the Lord's supper. In 1 Corinthians, the phrase is used for this purpose, *"Is not the bread which we break a sharing in the body of Christ."* 1 COR. 10:16B. Here, the word for sharing is that familiar Greek word, koinōnia. Acts 20 uses the same phrase, *"And on the first day of the week, when we were gathered together to break bread"*, ACTS 20:7. Here, the reference is also to the Lord's Supper. Thus, we have to conclude that the third activity of the early church was the regular observance of the Lord's Supper.

(d) They were continually devoting themselves to prayer – keeping in close touch with the Master. The word used here is the general word for worshipful prayer.

The Didache (120 AD) introduces another term that we may be unaccustomed to seeing, *"But on the Lord's own day gather yourselves together and break bread and give thanks, first confessing your transgressions, that your sacrifice may be pure.."*[53] The term, *"giving thanks"* is a phrase with a very specific meaning. The Greek for this phrase is eucharisteō (εὐχαριστέω), from which we get the word eucharist, the definition of which is communion. Thus, the term, *"giving thanks"*, used frequently by early church writers, referred to the communion service.

DAY OF THE MEETING
We are now in a position to examine which day the early Christians chose for meeting. In Acts 20, Luke writes, *"And on the first day of the week, when we were gathered together to break bread,"* ACTS 20:7. Thus, they met on the first day of the week. (Sunday is the first day of the week). In 1 Corinthians, Paul expects them to present their gifts on the first day, *"On the first day of every week let each one of you put aside and save, as he may prosper, that no collections be made when I come."* 1 COR. 16:2. In Revelation, John refers to a day called the Lord's Day, *"I was in the Spirit on the Lord's day, and I heard behind me a loud voice like the sound of a trumpet,"* REV. 1:10. All of

---

[53] *Didache*, Ch. 14

the early writers agreed that the Lord's day was the first day (Sunday). This position is supported by the Didache (120 AD), *"But on the Lord's own day gather yourselves together"* [54] Ignatius (106 AD) tells us why he met on the Lord's Day, *"no longer observing the Sabbath, but living in the observance of the Lord's Day, on which also our life has sprung up again by Him and by His death"*[55] Origen (240 AD) agreed, *"If it be objected to us on this subject that we ourselves are accustomed to observe certain days, as for example the Lord's day, the Preparation, the Passover, or Pentecost."* [56] To these we could add the writings of Tertullian (207 AD), Cyprian (250 AD), Clement of Alexandria (200 AD), and many others. The church fathers universally preached and practiced meeting on the first day of the week and universally referred to this day as the Lord's day. There is no support for observing any other day for the Christian. But why did they observe the First day? There are several reasons outlined by the early writers:

1. Jesus rose on the first day of the week
2. In John 20:26, the disciples gathered together after the Lord's death on the first day of the week
3. Pentecost and the start of the church occurred on the first day of the week, Acts 2:1.

Today, a few churches have departed from the day observed by early Christians, even though the Bible and early writers unanimously support the Lord's day.

---

[54] *Didache,* Ch 14
[55] Ignatius, *Epistle to the Magnesians,* Ch. 9
[56] Origen, *Against Celsus,* Book 8, ch. 22

WHAT DID THEY DO WHEN THEY MET?

It was apparent from the beginning that the main purpose in having the Lord's day meeting was to observe the Lord's supper. Luke writes in Acts, *"And on the first day of the week, when we were gathered together to break bread,"* ACTS 20:7. They gathered together to break bread — to observe the Lord's death and resurrection as He had commanded. This was not unexpected, for in 1 Corinthians Paul quotes Jesus, *" 'This is My body, which is for you; do this in remembrance of Me.' In the same way He took the cup also, after supper, saying, 'This cup is the new covenant in My blood; do this, as often as you drink it, in remembrance of Me.' For as often as you eat this bread and drink the cup, you proclaim the Lord's death until He comes."* 1 COR. 11:24-26. Thus, Christ expected us to observe His death and the early Christians carried out His wishes.

In Acts 6, we noted that the church offered public meals every day, including the Lord's day. It was common in Jerusalem to take the Lord's supper on the Lord's day after this meal. Paul alluded to this in 1 Corinthians, when he wrote, *"Therefore when you meet together, it is not to eat the Lord's Supper, for in your eating each one takes his own supper first; and one is hungry and another is drunk. What! Do you not have houses in which to eat and drink? Or do you despise the church of God, and shame those who have nothing? What shall I say to you? Shall I praise you? In this I will not praise you."* 1 COR. 11:20-22. They were being gluttonous and selfish at these dinners, and holding the Lord's supper in disrespect. Paul then goes on to instruct them further.

In other accounts, no dinner is mentioned. One of the earliest of writings, the Didache (120 AD), records, *"But every Lord's day do ye gather yourselves together, and break bread, and give thanksgiving after having confessed your transgressions, that your sacrifice may be pure."*[57] This makes

---

[57] *Didache*, Ch. 14

it apparent that they met for the primary purpose of having the Lord's supper. Note that this was done *every* Lord's day, the same as was done in Acts 20:7. Thus, both the Bible and church fathers put the Lord's supper at the center of worship. Today, many, many churches have departed from this practice of His Church, preferring to set their own schedule for the Lords supper: once per month, once per quarter, once per year, or never. Thus, they cease *"proclaiming the Lord's death"* every week to all as the Lord instructed us to do.

Several parts of present-day services are notably absent from that mentioned in the Didache. First, no praying is mentioned. We can speculate that praying did occur, but it was not mentioned. Second, there is no mention of reading the scriptures, teaching, singing, or collecting. However, in Acts 20, not only did the Christians have the Lord's supper, but Paul preached to them. Matthew writes concerning the first Lord's supper where Jesus and His Apostles were present, *"And after singing a hymn, they went out to the Mount of Olives."* MATT. 26:30. Thus, there was singing at the first Lord's Supper.

Later on in church history, writers indicate that there was a more extensive service. In a chapter titled, *"Weekly Worship of the Christians,"* Justin Martyr (150 AD) writes, *"And on the day called Sunday, all who live in cities or in the country gather together to one place, and the memoirs of the apostles or the writings of the prophets are read, as long as time permits; then, when the reader has ceased, the president* [the person who is presiding] *verbally instructs, and exhorts to the imitation of these good things. Then we all rise together and pray, and, as we before said, when our prayer is ended, bread and wine and water are brought, and the president in like manner offers prayers and thanksgivings, according to his ability, and the people assent, saying Amen; and there is a distribution to each, and a participation of that over which thanks have been given, and to those who are absent a portion is sent by the deacons.*

And they who are well to do, and willing, give what each thinks fit; and what is collected is deposited with the president, who succors the orphans and widows and those who, through sickness or any other cause, are in want, and those who are in bonds and the strangers sojourning among us, and in a word takes care of all who are in need. But Sunday is the day on which we all hold our common assembly, because it is the first day on which God, having wrought a change in the darkness and matter, made the world; and Jesus Christ our Savior on the same day rose from the dead. For He was crucified on the day before that of Saturn (Saturday); and on the day after that of Saturn, which is the day of the Sun, having appeared to His apostles and disciples, He taught them these things, which we have submitted to you also for your consideration." [58] According to this record, their service consisted of: reading scripture, teaching, praying, Lord's supper, and a collection. The scripture reading was from the Old Testament or from the writings of the apostles. It is apparent from this practice that the New Testament writings were now being accepted as scripture.

The president, the person presiding, then commented on the reading. He probably exhorted people to follow the teaching, relating it to other scriptures. Next, the people rose and prayed together. This was probably a unison-type prayer, since, later in the passage, the president is said to pray by himself over the communion emblems.

Their communion emblems consisted of bread, wine, and water. Justin Martyr explains that the wine is served mixed with water,[59] a custom, no doubt, borrowed from the Jewish observance of Passover.[60] In contrast to Justin Martyr and other post-Biblical writings, it should be noted that the Bible never

---

[58] Justin Martyr, *First Apology,* Ch. 67

[59] Justyn Martyr, *First Apology,* Ch. 65

[60] According to the Misnah, the Jewish commentary on the first five books of the Old Testament, the reason for mixing these liquids during Passover observance was that wine was considered too strong to be drunk by itself.

refers to the communion liquid as wine; it always calls it, "fruit of the vine," even though there is a word for wine in the Greek.

A collection, accepted only from those who were willing, is taken to help out the less fortunate. Note that there was no singing mentioned in the passage.

What, then, should His Church do when they meet? First, the centerpiece of the worship service should be the Lord's supper. He has commanded it and we have ample evidence that the early church practiced it every Lord's day. Second, reading the scriptures, teaching, and prayers can be part of the service. Third, singing was a part of the first Lord's supper. Fourth, a dinner could precede the worship activities. We shall examine the role of the collection more closely in the next section.

THE COLLECTION OF TITHES AND OFFERINGS

To examine the collection, we have to go to the Old Testament. Moses instituted a collection to build the tabernacle in Exodus, *"And Moses spoke to all the congregation of the sons of Israel, saying, 'This is the thing which the Lord has commanded, saying, "Take from among you a contribution to the Lord; whoever is of a willing heart, let him bring it as the Lord's contribution:"''"* EX. 35:4-5. The prerequisite to giving was "a willing heart." This theme is repeated over and over, *"everyone whose heart stirred him and everyone whose spirit moved him"*, EX. 35:21; *"And all the women whose heart stirred with a skill,"* EX. 35:26; *"all the men and women, whose heart moved them,"* EX. 35:29; and *"everyone whose heart stirred him,"* EX. 36:2. Thus, the prerequisite to God accepting their gift is that it had to be given from a willing heart. Today, the prerequisite to your giving a gift and the prerequisite to the church accepting a gift is that it has to be given from a willing heart. It has to be a *free will* offering. It cannot be coerced.

When King Jehoash became King of Judah, he wanted to establish a special collection so that the temple could be repaired.   To do this, he turned to Jehoiada, the priest, *"But Jehoiada the priest took a chest and bored a hole in its lid, and put it beside the altar, on the right side as one comes into the house of the Lord; and the priests who guarded the threshold put in it all the money which was brought into the house of the Lord."* 2 KINGS 12:9. This was the same treasure chest that Jesus was observing in Mark when he saw the widow put in her two pennies, *"And He sat down opposite the treasury, and began observing how the multitude were putting money into the treasury;"* MARK 12:41. This satisfied the requirement that giving must be from a willing heart. The widow was not coerced — she gave out of a willing heart.

Paul preaches this same theme to the Corinthians, *"Let each one do just as he has purposed in his heart; not grudgingly or under compulsion; for God loves a cheerful giver."* 2 COR. 9:7. Again, the emphasis is on willing givers. The Greek word for "grudgingly" means "pain in body or mind, grief, sorrow"; the Greek word for "compulsion" is "of necessity." Thus, we are to freely give — free from any regret and free from any arm twisting. We get the English word, hilarious, from the Greek word used here for "cheerful." Therefore, our giving must be free from compulsion and it must come from our will. That is what *free will* means!!

Paul then provides a very telling verse in 1 Corinthians, *"On the first day of every week let each one of you put aside and save, as he may prosper, that no collections be made when I come."* 1 COR. 16:2.   The Greek wording means, "that there may not be, when I come, collections going on then."   Paul *avoided* collections!!   They were a waste of his time and effort. He did not want there to be any collections going on there while he was visiting Corinth.   If this is true, then how were the people to get their donations to him? Paul was a Jew. He knew the tradition of the temple.   It is very probable that he did exactly as Jehoiada did, exactly as Jesus observed. He probably had a box with a hole in the top and asked people *whose heart was stirred* to place their funds within the box. It was that simple.

But was the collection a part of the actual worship service conducted by Paul? It is highly probable that it was not. It is not even mentioned in one of the earliest documents, the Didache (120 AD). Their emphasis was on the Lord's supper. It is mentioned in Justin Martyr's description of the worship service (150 AD). However, even there, he says, *"And they who are well to do, and willing, give what each thinks fit; and what is collected is deposited with the president,"* [61] Note his emphasis on being willing.

Apostolic Constitutions (350 AD) seems to indicate that a person's tithe and offerings were separate from the worship service, also. Part of it was to be given to the priest, and part to the widows and orphans.[62] However, this document makes it very clear that offerings were to be refused from certain people, such as corrupt dealers, fornicators, extortionists, thieves, unjust public officials, drunkards, usurers, and many others.[63] It goes on to say that if offerings are gathered from such people, that these offerings are to be destroyed. *"But if at any time you be forced unwillingly to receive money from any ungodly person, lay it out in wood and coals, that so neither the widow nor the orphan may receive any of it, or be forced to buy with it either meat or drink, which it is unfit to do."* [64] They felt so strongly that offerings must be given from a willing, pure heart, that they would destroy them before they would use them.

This same philosophy was adopted by St. Patrick of Ireland (460 AD). He states, *"And many gifts were offered to me in sorrow and tears, and I offended the donors, much against*

---

[61] Justin Martyr, *First Apology,* Ch. 67

[62] *Apostolic Constitutions,* Book 7, Ch. 29

[63] *Apostolic Constitutions,* Book 4, Ch. 6

[64] *Apostolic Constitutions,* Book 4, Ch. 10

the wishes of some of my seniors; but, guided by God, in no way did I agree with them or acquiesce." [65]   People of impure hearts were begging him to accept their gifts, but he refused, because their heart was not right with God.

Commodianus (240 AD) also, considers such gifts as worthless, *"One gives gifts that he may make another of no account; or if thou has lent on usury, taking twenty-four percent, thou wishest to bestow charity that thou mayest purge thyself, as being evil, with that which is evil. The Almighty absolutely rejects such works as these."* [66]

What does all of this mean to today's church about collections?   Many churches have become accustomed to passing a plate in order to receive their collections. I have seen guests at such churches rifle through their pockets in order to give something. They were not giving out of a willing heart; they were giving out of compulsion.   Even though I give regularly, there have been times when I visited other churches and felt compelled to give because a plate was passed in front of me. I suggest that this is not His Plan. I suggest that He wants us, as His servants, to assure that all gifts are given freely. I suggest that we go back to what King Jehoash did, to what Jesus observed, and to what Paul did: to placing a box where people can deposit their offerings. Only in this way can the church assure that it is given of free will.

Furthermore, the church should be careful when it pleads for funds from the pulpit. Remember that these funds need to be from acceptable sources, from those of pure heart and those of free will. Remember, also, that the central focus of the worship service should be on the Lord's supper. If pleading for funds takes away from that goal, then the pleading should cease. In addition, having such things as rummage sales, bake sales, and other money raising efforts does not conform with the

---

[65] *Confession of St. Patrick*
[66] Commodianus, *Instructions,* Ch. 65

examples of free will offerings given within the Bible. On the contrary, they are mercenary acts.

A few years ago, a roving Christian drama troupe came to the church and put on a performance. Attendance usually ran about 100 for this congregation. Prior to the performance, I met with the leader of the troupe and he inquired about our taking an offering to defray expenses — which we had promised to do. I assured him that a special love offering would be announced from the pulpit, and the church would, as they always did, deposit such funds in the boxes at the rear of the auditorium. When he heard this, you could see his countenance drop. He was accustomed to having the plate passed. However, when the evening was done, the congregation had presented them with over $400 in their offerings — the largest he had received from any church they had visited. Christians do not have to be coerced into giving.

MUSIC AS PART OF THE WORSHIP SERVICE

We first note that music was used extensively in the Old Testament, both vocal and instrumental music. In the New Testament, we have several examples of Paul's teachings and practice about music, not especially related to times when the church assembled. Paul and Silas sang hymns of praise to God while they were imprisoned, ACTS 16:25. Paul advises us to continue, *"speaking to one another in psalms and hymns and spiritual songs, singing and making melody with your heart to the Lord;"* EPH. 5:19. He further advises us, *"Let the word of Christ richly dwell within you, with all wisdom teaching and admonishing one another with psalms and hymns and spiritual songs, singing with thankfulness in your hearts to God."* COL. 3:16.

Thus, in these examples, we find three types of songs mentioned: psalms, hymns, and spiritual songs. The word, psalm, comes from the Greek, psalmos (ψαλμός). It meant a striking or twitching with the fingers, as on a musical instrument, rather than with a pick. Indeed, there are numerous references by the early writers referring to a harp-like musical instrument called a psaltery.[67] Thus, in the New Testament, the psalm to which Paul referred was a praise to God accompanied by a musical instrument in the tradition of David. A hymn is a song praising God. Our present day "praise songs" would fall into this category. A spiritual song is a song with a spiritual meaning. The melody may have been secular, and spiritual words added, for example.

We have two specific instances of the use of music during the assembly. First, Jesus and the Apostles sang a hymn before going to Gethsemane in Matt. 26:30. Second, Paul advises that, *"When you assemble, each one has a psalm, has a teaching, has a revelation, has a tongue, has an interpretation. Let all things be done for edification."* 1 COR 14:26. What do these verses tell us? Hymns and psalms were used during worship. (Psalms, by their very nature, implied that instruments were used). However, all three types — hymns, psalms, and spiritual songs — were used at other times.

Let us now examine the writings of the church fathers. Ignatius (106 AD) uses the example of the harp several times when referring to how the officers of the church should harmonize.[68] Justin Martyr (150 AD) criticizes the Greeks for *"excessive banquetings, and subtle flutes which provoke to lustful movements"* [69] Later, though, he compares righteous men to a harp or a lyre.[70] Clement of Alexandria (200 AD) waxes poetic as he sings of Christianity, *"The righteous are the chorus; the music is a hymn of the King of the universe. The*

---

[67] Some of these speak of it being used in a debauching manner, such as Irenaeus, *Against Heresies,* Book 4, Ch. 2. Others speak of it as being used in a Godly manner, such as Cyprian, *On the Public Shows,* Ch. 4.
[68] Ignatius, *Epistle to the Ephesians,* Ch. 4 and *Epistle to the Philadelphians,* Ch. 1
[69] Justin Martyr, *Dialogue of Justin with Trypho,* Ch. 4
[70] Justin Martyr, *Dialogue of Justin with Trypho,* Ch. 8

*maidens strike the lyre, the angels praise, the prophets speak;
the sound of music issues forth, they run and pursue the jubilant
band; those that are called make haste, eagerly desiring to
receive the Father."* [71]   He encourages use of musical
instruments in praise to God, *"For the apostle adds again,
'Teaching and admonishing one another in all wisdom, in
psalms, and hymns, and spiritual songs, singing with grace in
your heart to God.' And again, 'Whatsoever ye do in word or
deed, do all in the name of the Lord Jesus, giving thanks to God
and His Father.' This is our thankful revelry. And even if you
wish to sing and play to the harp or lyre, there is no blame. ...
and let our songs be hymns to God. 'Let them praise,' it is said,
'His name in the dance, and let them play to Him on the timbrel
and psaltery.' And what is the choir which plays? The Spirit
will show thee: 'Let His praise be in the congregation (church)
of the saints; let them be joyful in their King.'"* [72]

What is the conclusion to the matter of music during a
worship service?   Although the primary emphasis of the
worship service was on the Lord's supper, both singing and
instrumental music were used very early in church history
during the worship service. Writers encouraged its use for the
praise of God and discouraged its use in ungodly situations.
This can be compared with today. We have the opportunity to
use music to the glory of God, or we can use it in an ungodly
manner.

SUMMARY

Worship service of the early church centered on the
Lord's Supper. They met to celebrate His sin-cleansing death
and to declare to the world that He is coming again. They also
included reading the scripture, teaching, and prayer. Music was
also a part of some of the services. Although donations were

---

[71] Clement of Alexandria, *Exhortation to the Heathen*, Ch. 12
[72] Clement of Alexandria, *The Instructor*, Book 2, Ch. 4

collected, the offering was not a usual part of the service. Collections were avoided as a distraction.

Chapter 9

SALVATION OF CHRIST'S CHURCH

INTRODUCTION

One of the most controversial subjects in today's church is that of salvation. How are we saved and what must we do to be saved? Unlike the divisions today, the early church was united in answering this question. Let us first examine the Bible, then these early writers.

SALVATION IN THE BIBLE

I once had a young lady ask me, "What must I do to be saved?" I could have picked some verses out of the Bible and "led her down the garden path," but these would have been my ideas. I wanted the Holy Spirit to move her — not me. Therefore, instead of answering the question myself, I asked her to thumb through the Book of Acts, and make a list of what steps each of the people in Acts followed in order to be saved. The list came out as follows:

Location	Case	Steps followed
Acts 2:1+	Day of Pentecost	Heard, believed in Christ, repented, were baptized
Acts 8:12-13	People of Samaria	Heard, believed, baptized
Acts 8:26+	Ethiopian Eunuch	Heard, baptized, [believed, confessed, see footnote] [73]
Acts 9:1+	Paul	Heard, believed, confessed[74], repented, baptized

---

[73] The earliest manuscripts of the Bible omit verse 37, the confession. Vs. 37 also states *"he believed."*
[74] See Acts 9:20

Acts 10:34	Cornelius, etc.	Heard, believed, baptized
Acts 16:14+	Lydia, etc.	Heard, believed, baptized
Acts 16:31+	Jailor, etc	Heard, believed, baptized
Acts 18:8+	Corinthians	Heard, believed, baptized
Acts 19:1+	Ephesians	Heard, believed, baptized

What conclusions can I draw from this chart? Every one of these persons heard the Word of God, believed that Jesus was the Christ, and they were baptized. I assume they also repented of their sins and confessed that Jesus was the Christ. Thus, it seems simple to me that this is God's plan for salvation.

I could easily point to one scripture, pull it out of context, and prove a different plan. For example, I could pull out, *"For God so loved the world, that He gave His only begotten Son, that whoever believes in Him should not perish, but have eternal life."* JOHN 3:16. Aha! Only belief is required. Or, I could pull out another scripture, *"that if you confess with your mouth Jesus as Lord, and believe in your heart that God raised Him from the dead, you shall be saved."* ROM. 10:9. Aha! Confession and belief are required. Or, I could pull out another scripture, *"For we maintain that a man is justified by faith apart from works of the Law."* ROM. 3:28. Aha! Faith is required.

All of this reminds me of the time I went to the county to find out what was required to build a house. When I visited the Health Department, they told me a sewer permit was required. When I visited the Ecology Department, they told me a well permit was required. When I visited the County Building Department, they told me a building permit was required. When I visited the State Labor and Industries Department, they told me an electrical permit was required. In truth, all were required in order to build the house. In like manner, if we consider what the entire New Testament says about building God's house, rather than focusing on one particular verse, we will get an accurate picture of what God wants for us to be saved.   In addition to this, when we then examine what was actually practiced in Acts, we reach the conclusion that they heard, believed, confessed, repented, and were baptized.

HEAR

The Book of Romans tells us, *"For 'Whoever will call upon the name of the Lord will be saved.'   How then shall they call upon Him in whom they have not believed? And how shall they believe in Him whom they have not heard? And how shall they hear without a preacher?   And how shall they preach unless they are sent? Just as it is written, 'How beautiful are the feet of those who bring glad tidings of good things!' However, they did not all heed the glad tidings; for Isaiah says, 'Lord, who has believed our report?'   So faith comes from hearing, and hearing by the word of Christ."* ROM. 10:13-17.

Thus, God's Plan for Salvation starts with a preacher preaching His word.   Tertullian (207 AD) notes that preaching must occur prior to baptism. *"For preaching is the prior thing, baptizing the posterior."* [75]   The preacher's preaching then results in our part, hearing the word; which, in turn, results in our believing the Word; and, finally, culminates in our calling on His Name. Notice that the first thing *we* have to do is hear. This is the Greek word, akouō, (ἀκούω), from which we get the English word acoustic. Its meaning is the same as in English, to hear.

BELIEVE

The next step in the process is to believe. *"that if you confess with your mouth Jesus as Lord, and believe in your heart that God raised Him from the dead, you shall be saved."* ROM. 10:9. The word for *"believe"* comes from the Greek word, pisteuō (πιστεύω).   The meaning of this word is very interesting, as compared with the meaning of our English word,

---

[75] Tertullian, *On Baptism,* Ch. 14

"believe."   It is a term that means to be convinced by good evidence, such as that which would occur within a courtroom. Thus, we are to listen to the evidence that Jesus has presented and make our decision about Him.

The noun for this word is translated as "faith" in most Bibles. Therefore, belief and faith are exactly the same word in the original, and we should not try to separate their meanings based upon the English translation of the word. When we use the noun, faith, it also means a belief based upon evidence. However, we should NOT have, what I refer to as, "blind faith." Our faith should be rooted in evidence.

I once had two gentlemen appear at my door, declaring themselves to be elders of the Mormon Church. They asked me if I would like to have a copy of the Book of Mormon. I told them, "I have a copy. Let me study it and come back in two weeks." I then studied the book and made some notes. Third Nephi in the Book of Mormon, contains the same multiple manuscript variations that the King James Version contains[76], and many of these variations did not occur until several hundred years after Christ.[77] Based upon this internal evidence, it was

---

[76] In 1611, when the King James Version (KJV) was made, the translators based their work on Greek from 10-12th century manuscripts.   A large number of earlier manuscripts were discovered in the latter half of the 19th. century.   Thus, later versions of the Bible, such as the New American Standard Version, the New International Version, and the Revised Standard Version, were based upon earlier manuscripts than the KJV.   Since there were some textual variations between the earlier and the later manuscripts, the KJV and later versions differ in some of their wording.

[77] (a) 3 Nephi 12:9, *"children"* is same as KJV, Matt. 5:9. Greek from earlier manuscripts has *"sons."* (b) 3 Nephi 12:27 has *"of old time"*, same as KJV, Matt. 5:27. Early Greek manuscripts omit the phrase. (c) 3 Nephi 13:13 has *"For Thine is the kingdom and the power, and the glory forever. Amen.",* same as KJV, Matt. 6:13. NASB footnotes it because this phrase does not occur in the earliest manuscripts. Moreover, Tertullian (207 AD) discusses the Lord's Prayer, clause by clause, in his commentary, *"On Prayer."* In a chapter titled, *"The Seventh or Final Clause,"* he omits this phrase, declaring that the final clause is *"Lead us not into temptation.".* There are many other examples in 3 Nephi of KJV variations.

apparent to me that the Book of Mormon was not written at the time of Christ as its proponents have advocated.

When the "elders" returned, I shared this with them and asked them to explain how this was possible. They could not explain it, but ended up asking me to have faith. Here, they were speaking of a blind faith — one that could overcome the obvious contrary manuscript evidence. I quoted 3 Nephi 23:1, "And now, behold, I say unto you, that ye ought to search these things." I told them, "I searched, and they were not true." We are not told to have blind faith in Jesus.

CONFESS

Sometimes we get confused about whether this term means to confess our sins or to confess Christ. Romans 10:9, quoted previously, makes it clear that we are to confess Christ. The confession of Peter, *"And Simon Peter answered and said, 'Thou art the Christ, the Son of the living God.'"* MATT. 16:16. is called, by many, "the Good Confession." I believe it is a model for what Jesus wants us to confess. *"Everyone therefore who shall confess Me before men, I will also confess him before My Father who is in heaven."* MATT. 10:32.

The word for confess in the Greek is homologeō (ὁμολογέω). The "homo" means "the same" and the "logeō" means "to speak." This, it means to speak the same thing, to agree. The basic question is, then, do you agree that "Jesus is Lord?" Do you agree that *"Jesus is the Christ, the Son of the Living God?"* If so, you should confess this publicly.

REPENT

After Peter preached his sermon on the day of Pentecost, those present asked, *"what shall we do?"* Peter replied, *"Repent ... and be baptized."* ACTS 2:37-38. Thus, repentance was a part of God's Plan for these listeners to be saved. The Greek word for "to repent" is metanoeō (μετανοέω). The "meta" means "after" (implying change) and the "noeō" means "the mind." Thus, it means "to change one's mind or purpose." No longer is our purpose to serve ourselves, our new purpose is the serve Christ. We cannot have Him as Master and have ourselves as master in our lives. One, and only One — Jesus — must become the Head of our lives. The question, then, that we need to answer is, are we willing to change our lives and put Christ first? Are we willing to allow Him and His Word to guide us in everything we say and in everything we do?

Tertullian (207 AD) notes that repentance must occur prior to baptism (which he notes washes our sins away and admits us to eternal life). *"We are not washed in order that we may cease sinning, but because we have ceased, since in heart we have been bathed already."* [78] Thus, repentance is an essential element in God's plan of salvation and, once accomplished, can then lead us to baptism.

BE BAPTIZED

The usual controversy is that of baptism. Some modern day theologians say, "Baptism is a work — and we cannot work ourselves into salvation. It comes from God's grace." I will not argue that salvation is from God's grace — it is. However, what was actually done by people to receive salvation in the New Testament? In every case they were baptized.

The word, baptize, comes from a Greek word baptizō (βαπτίζω). It means to "plunge, dip, or immerse." In classical Greek, it was used to describe ships that had been sunk. It was also used to describe cloths that were to be dyed when they were plunged into a vat of dye. Baptizō was never used to mean, "sprinkle." That is another Greek word which is, in fact, used in the New Testament. Look at Hebrews, *"let us draw near with a sincere heart in full assurance of faith, having our hearts sprinkled clean from an evil conscience and our bodies washed with pure water."* HEB. 10:22. In this passage, the Greek

---

[78] Tertullian, *On Repentence,* Ch. 6

word for "sprinkle" is rhantizō (ῥαντίζω). Note that it is a completely different word from baptizō.

The English word, baptize, was coined during the seventeenth century. In 1611, when the King James Version was written, the translators wanted to obtain the favor of the king, which was required in order to get it published. If they translated baptizō as "immerse," they would incur his disfavor, for the King was from a church that sprinkled. If they translated it, "sprinkle," they would be intellectually dishonest. Therefore, to solve this problem, they invented a new word, baptize. No one could argue with use of this word. The original, Greek word used in the New Testament, however, had only one meaning: to plunge, dip or immerse. It did NOT mean "sprinkle."

Early Church Writers on Baptism

What did baptism mean to the early church writers? Let us take them, in chronological order, one at a time.

The Epistle of Barnabus (75 AD) records, *"Concerning the water, indeed, it is written, in reference to the Israelites, that they should not receive that baptism which leads to the remission of sins, but should procure another for themselves. ... This meaneth, that we indeed descend into the water full of sins and defilement, but come up, bearing fruit in our heart, having the fear [of God] and trust in Jesus in our spirit."*[79] Thus, there is a baptism which leads to remission of sins. However, the Israelites did not have access to it. Furthermore, he declares that baptism cleanses us from our sins.

Ignatius (106 AD) says, *"Let your baptism endure as your arms; your faith as your helmet; your love as your spear; your patience as a complete panoply."* [80] Thus, he expected every believer to be baptized.

---

[79] *Epistle of Barnabus*, Ch. 11
[80] Ignatius, *Epistle to Polycarp*, Ch. 6

The Shepherd of Hermas (140 AD) recounts, *"And I said to him, 'I should like to continue my questions.' 'Speak on,' said he. And I said, 'I heard, sir, some teachers maintain that there is no other repentance than that which takes place, when we descended into the water and received remission of our former sins.' He said to me, 'That was sound doctrine which you heard; for that is really the case. For he who has received remission of his sins ought not to sin any more, but to live in purity.'"* [81]   Thus, according to the Shepherd, remission of sins occurs in baptism.

Justin Martyr (150 AD). declares, *"Then they are brought by us where there is water, and are regenerated in the same manner in which we were ourselves regenerated. For, in the name of God, the Father and Lord of the universe, and of our Savior Jesus Christ, and of the Holy Spirit, they then receive the washing with water. ... And for this [rite] we have learned from the apostles this reason. Since at our birth we were born without our own knowledge or choice, by our parents coming together, and were brought up in bad habits and wicked training; in order that we may not remain the children of necessity and of ignorance, but may become the children of choice and knowledge, and may obtain in the water the remission of sins formerly committed, there is pronounced over him who chooses to be born again, and has repented of his sins, the name of God the Father and Lord of the universe."* [82] Thus, we are regenerated and our sins are remitted (taken away) in baptism. Note further, that only those who can choose — adults and youth — are capable of being baptized.

Irenaeus (185 AD), in *Against Heresies,* recounts the conversions in the Book of Acts, much as I did in the preceding

---

[81] *Shepherd of Hermas,* Book 2, Commandment Fourth, Ch. 3
[82] Justin Martyr, *First Apology,* Ch. 61. This chapter is entitled "Christian Baptism."

part of this chapter, noting that each was baptized.[83]   He then comments on Paul's conversion, *"Paul himself also — after that the Lord spoke to him out of heaven, and showed him that, in persecuting His disciples, he persecuted his own Lord, and sent Ananias to him that he might recover his sight, and be baptized — preached ..."* [84]   In another of his writings, he spoke of Naaman's cleansing, *"'And dipped himself,' says [the Scripture], 'seven times in Jordan.' It was not for nothing that Naaman of old, when suffering from leprosy, was purified upon his being baptized, but [it served] as an indication to us. For as we are lepers in sin, we are made clean, by means of the sacred water and the invocation of the Lord, from our old transgressions; being spiritually regenerated as new-born babes, even as the Lord has declared: 'Except a man be born again through water and the Spirit, he shall not enter into the kingdom of heaven.'"* [85]   According to him, we are made clean, that is, regenerated, by baptism.

Clement of Alexandria (200 AD) declares, *"then, those who have shaken off sleep forthwith become all awake within; or rather, as those who try to remove a film that is over the eyes, do not supply to them from without the light which they do not possess, but removing the obstacle from the eyes, leave the pupil free; thus also we who are baptized, having wiped off the sins which obscure the light of the Divine Spirit.   ...   In the same way, therefore, we also, repenting of our sins, renouncing our iniquities, purified by baptism, speed back to the eternal light"* [86]   Thus, he, too, believes that sins are washed away in baptism.   In Chapter 12, he says, *"The view I take is, that He Himself formed man of the dust, and regenerated him by water."* [87]

---

[83] Irenaeus, *Against Heresies,* Book 3, Ch. 12
[84] Irenaeus, *Against Heresies,* Book 3, Ch. 12:9.
[85] Irenaeus, *Fragments from His Lost Writings,* Ch. 34
[86] Clement of Alexandria, Book 1, *The Instructor,* Ch. 6
[87] Clement of Alexandria, Book 1, *The Instructor,* Ch. 12

Tertullian (207 AD) has an entire discourse on baptism. His first sentence is, *"Happy is our sacrament of water, in that, by washing away the sins of our early blindness, we are set free and admitted into eternal life!"* [88] He had no doubt that sins were remove in baptism by the grace of the Lord. This same writer produces evidence that, not only did Christians know that baptism resulted in salvation, but even non-believers did. He records the following martyrdom, *"And immediately at the conclusion of the exhibition he [Saturus] was thrown to the leopard; and with one bite of his, he was bathed with such a quantity of blood, that the people shouted out to him as he was returning, the testimony of his second baptism, 'Saved and washed, saved and washed.'"* [89] The heathen crowd, reveling in the gory deaths of Saturus, Perpetua, and Felicitas by wild beasts, mocked these martyrs with an epithet that revealed that even they knew that salvation came through baptism.

I do not know how many examples I need to supply. Every early church writer believed the same — that our sins are taken away by Christ's grace through our baptism. Furthermore, only adults can be baptized, for only they are capable of repenting and of confessing Christ as Savior. How much clearer can the scriptures be? Part of God's plan for salvation is the washing away of our sins by His Grace through baptism.

We should note that every person was baptized as soon as they made a decision for Christ. They did not wait until Sunday, wait until Easter, or wait for any other reason. Baptism took place *immediately*. We need to follow this example.

Many churches today have completely changed baptism from its original method and purpose. First, some sprinkle, contrary to the scripture which says to immerse. Second, some

---

[88] Tertullian, *On Baptism,* Ch. 1
[89] Tertullian, *The Passion of the Holy Martyrs Perpetua and Felicitas,*   Ch. 6:4

sprinkle infants. A requirement of baptism is that you repent.
A child cannot repent; therefore he cannot be baptized. Look at
the writings of the early church authors. Every one of them
believed in adult immersion. There was only one variation: a
few dipped the baptizee three times: once for the Father, once
for the Son, and once for the Holy Spirit.[90]

Many churches have perverted what baptism means.
Some baptize to "join" the local church. Baptism in His Church
was done to remove sins — not to join a church. He adds us to
His Church automatically when we are baptized.

Others baptize, supposedly, after we have been saved.
The writings of the early church make it clear that our sins are
removed during baptism. We are saved once we have been
baptized, not baptized once we have been saved.

WALK THE WALK

The Bible makes it clear that we are expected to follow
Christ AFTER we have been baptized into Him. The writer of
Hebrews admonishes, *"Let love of the brethren continue. Do
not neglect to show hospitality to strangers, for by this some
have entertained angels without knowing it. Remember the
prisoners, as though in prison with them, and those who are ill-
treated, since you yourselves also are in the body. Let marriage
be held in honor among all, and let the marriage bed be
undefiled; for fornicators and adulterers God will judge. 5 Let
your character be free from the love of money, being content
with what you have; for He Himself has said, 'I will never
desert you, nor will I ever forsake you,'"* HEB. 13:1-5. Note that,
if we follow this plan, God will never desert us.

One of my favorite verses is in Philippians, where Paul
addresses how positive we can be as Christians if we direct our
attention to the things of God. *"Finally, brethren, whatever is
true, whatever is honorable, whatever is right, whatever is pure,*

---

[90] Tertullian, *Against Praxeas*, Ch. 26 and *Apostolic Constitutions*, Ch. 7

whatever is lovely, whatever is of good repute, if there is any excellence and if anything worthy of praise, let your mind dwell on these things.   The things you have learned and received and heard and seen in me, practice these things; and the God of peace shall be with you."   PHIL. 4:8-9   From the above two passages, it can be seen that we are expected to live holy lives. If we do this, God will not desert us.

Can We Desert God After We are Saved?

But we're always looking for the escape clause. "What happens if we fail to follow Him after we are saved?" Why are we asking this question at all? If He wants us to follow Him, let's do it. What part of "follow Me" do we not understand?

In spite of being told to follow Him, some will stray, eventually becoming lost. What happens then? In Luke, chapter 15, Christ gives three examples of the lost: a lost sheep, a lost coin, and a lost soul. First, He discusses a lost sheep. Note that the sheep decided to get lost and, as a result, was, indeed, lost. The Savior then went out to find him. The second example is similar. The coin was lost and was then found.

In the third example, a son decided to "lose" his father. In so doing, he was separated — lost — from the security and the knowledge of his father. Note that he did this on his own. The father did not lose him, he lost the father.

However, he then decided to return to his father. Note that it was his volition that got him going. Finally, he found his father. The father said of him, *"this brother of yours was dead and has begun to live, and was lost and has been found."*   LUKE 15:32. Thus, there is no doubt in our minds that the son was, first, alive, then dead, then alive again. Was it possible for him to lose the protection of his father? Absolutely!! He did it. From this example, we learn that Our Father will not desert us, but we can desert Him. The consequences of such a desertion are "lost-ness" and "dead-ness." Hmmm. Not a good state to contemplate.

The writings of the early authors are very clear about the necessity of maintaining holy lives. However, only a few comment on what happens if we turn our back on Christ after becoming one of His. Again, their emphasis is the same as that in the Bible. God tells us to be holy. Do it!!

Clement of Rome (95 AD) noted that, prior to their sinful act of dismissing their elders, the Corinthians led holy lives, *"Thus a profound and abundant peace was given to you all, and ye had an insatiable desire for doing good, while a full outpouring of the Holy Spirit was upon you all. Full of holy designs, ye did, with true earnestness of mind and a godly confidence, stretch forth your hands to God Almighty, beseeching Him to be merciful unto you, ... Ye were sincere and uncorrupted, and forgetful of injuries between one another. Every kind of faction and schism was abominable in your sight. ... Adorned by a thoroughly virtuous and religious life, ye did all things in the fear of God. The commandments and ordinances of the Lord were written upon the tablets of your hearts."* [91] Living holy was expected of all Christians.

Later in his letter, Clement of Rome (95 AD) exhorts these misguided Christians to repent of their sins, quoting the Old Testament, *"Though your sins be like crimson, I will make them white as snow; though they be like scarlet, I will whiten them like wool. And if ye be willing and obey Me, ye shall eat the good of the land; but if ye refuse, and will not hearken unto Me, the sword shall devour you, for the mouth of the Lord hath spoken these things."* [92] Thus, at this point in time, Clement considered them in danger of being devoured by God's sword. This is certainly not a saved state.

---

[91] Clement of Rome, *Epistle to the Corinthians,* Ch. 2
[92] Clement of Rome, *Epistle to the Corinthians,* Ch. 8 quoting Isaiah 1:18-20.

Justin Martyr (150 AD) is more explicit concerning desertion, *"And I hold, further, that such as have confessed and known this man to be Christ, yet who have gone back from some cause to the legal dispensation, and have denied that this man is Christ, and have repented not before death, shall by no means be saved."* [93]   Here, he clearly states that a person can deny Christ after he has confessed Christ, and, in so doing, will not be saved.

Tertullian states that a second repentance is in order after desertion. In a paragraph titled, "Of Repentance, in the Case of Such as Have Lapsed After Baptism", he states, *"You have what you now deserved not, for you had lost what you had received. If the Lord's indulgence grants you the means of restoring what you had lost, be thankful for the benefit renewed, not to say amplified; for 'restoring' is a greater thing than giving, inasmuch as 'having lost' is more miserable than never having received at all. However, if any do incur the debt of a second repentance, his spirit is not to be forthwith cut down and undermined by despair. Let it by all means be irksome to sin again, but let not to repent again be irksome: irksome to imperil one's self again, but not to be again set free. Let none be ashamed. Repeated sickness must have repeated medicine. You will show your gratitude to the Lord by not refusing what the Lord offers you. You have offended, but can still be reconciled. You have One whom you may satisfy, and Him willing."* [94]   It is very clear from this passage that Tertullian believed a Christian could leave Christ and have to be restored again.

OTHER SALVATION STRATEGIES ATTEMPTED

Modern Christianity has attempted to describe other means for salvation than the plan Christ laid out in His word.

---

[93] Justin Martyr, *Dialogue with Trypho,* Ch. 47
[94] Tertullian, *On Repentance,* Ch. 7

We shall now shine the light of His Word on several of these strategies.

Taking Jesus into Your Heart

Some would say that, to be saved, you should "take Jesus into your heart." The phrase, "in [or into] your heart" is used five times in the New Testament: three times in Rom. 10:6-9. The other times it does not refer to salvation. Paul declares, *"that if you confess with your mouth Jesus as Lord, and believe in your heart that God raised Him from the dead, you shall be saved; for with the heart man believes, resulting in righteousness, and with the mouth he confesses, resulting in salvation."* ROM. 10:9. The Greek meaning of the phrase "resulting in salvation" is, literally, "to salvation," meaning that it points toward salvation. It is not salvation itself, but points to salvation. I could use the same phrase by saying that my driveway leads to town. That is, it points to town. However, it is not, itself, town. As the book of Acts demonstrates, only when His plan of salvation is completed in baptism are we saved. Note that never once does anyone in the Bible tell us to "take Jesus into your heart." We should not use the phrase, either.

The phrases, "in your heart" or "into your heart" are completely foreign to the early church writers, as far as salvation goes. The Shepherd of Hermas (140 AD) speaks of either a good angel or a bad angel ascending "into your heart."[95] Tertullian (207 AD) expresses a similar idea.[96] We have already spoken of the testimony of these two authors that remission of sins comes through His Grace in baptism. All the early church writers say that salvation is completed through His Grace during baptism for the remission of our sins. Thus, the concept of being saved when we take Jesus into our heart is completely

---

[95] *Shepherd of Hermas, Sixth Commandment,* Ch. 2
[96] Tertullian, *On Idolatry,* Ch. 23

foreign to both the New Testament and the early church writers. Why do some people today still try to change God's plan into "their plan?"

Accepting Jesus as Christ

A second salvation strategy is to say that, when you "accept Jesus as Christ," you are saved. The phrase, "accept Jesus," is not used anywhere in the Bible. Furthermore, this phrase is used only three times by the Ante-Nicene Fathers: Origen indicates that Josephus does not accept Jesus as Christ.[97] Origen uses the term two times in referring to the heretic Celcius as having accepted Jesus as Christ, but rejecting Him by the teachings he professes.[98] We should also note that Satan accepts Jesus as Christ. Thus, "accepting Jesus" is not a Biblical phrase used to describe Christians.

On the other hand, the Bible does refer to God accepting us. In Gen. 4:9, Abel's sacrifice was accepted by God. In 2 Cor. 5:9, Paul desires to be accepted of Christ (KJV. NASB has "pleasing"). In Rom. 14:3, Paul indicates that those who eat vegetables and meat are accepted by God. Thus, if we are to use the term correctly, we should pray that we are accepted by God, not that we accept God. After all, who is the God and who is the servant in this relationship?

If we wish to describe those who have come to Christ, we can use the Biblical phrase, "baptized into Christ." It is used twice within the Bible. In Romans, Paul declares, *"Or do you not know that all of us who have been baptized into Christ Jesus have been baptized into His death?"* ROM. 6:3. In Galatians, he expands the definition, *"For all of you who were baptized into Christ have clothed yourselves with Christ."* GAL. 3:27. Thus, Christians are engulfed every day by the influence of Christ in their lives. This same phrase is very frequently quoted

---

[97] Origen, *Against Heresies,* Book 10, Ch. 17
[98] Origen, *Against Heresies,* Book 2, Ch. 3 and Book 5, Ch. 61

by the early writers to indicate those who have been saved.[99]
We should follow the examples in the Bible and emulate the
early writers by using this phrase to describe those who have
dedicated their lives to Christ.

Come to the Altar

Another salvation strategy that is used by some modern
churches is to "come to the altar," meaning a physical altar
within the church building. Matthew tells us to make friends
with our brother before we bring our offering to the altar, Matt.
5:23-24. Jesus was speaking to Jews, so He was obviously
referring to the altar at the temple. The Book of Hebrews
speaks of Jesus being our altar, Heb. 13:10. All other references
in the New Testament refer to the Jewish altar. There is never a
reference to bring our sins to the altar.

Polycarp (110 AD) speaks of widows being altars of God
as they lead Godly lives.[100] Ignatius (106 AD) speaks of the
church as being an altar.[101] Irenaeus (185 AD) speaks of our
offering things to the altar of God, indicating that that altar is in
heaven.[102] The Shepherd of Hermas (140 AD) indicates that the
wicked cannot ascend to the altar of God.[103] Felix (166-198 AD)
is very explicitly states that Christians do not have altars, *"Why
have they* [that is, the Christians] *no altars, no temples, no
acknowledged images?"* [104] We do not see an altar to which we
should come for salvation, unless that altar is the spiritual altar
of Christ Himself. The concept of coming to an altar to have
our sins forgiven is totally absent from both the Bible and the

---

[99] Clement of Alexander, *The Instructor,* Book 1, Ch. 6; Tertullian, *Against Marcion,* Book 3, Ch. 12, and others.
[100] Polycarp, *Epistle to the Philippians,* Ch. 4
[101] Ignatius, *Epistle to the Ephesians,* Ch. 5
[102] Irenaeus, *Against Heresies,* Book 4, Ch. 18
[103] *Shepherd of Hermas, Commandment Ten*
[104] *The Octavius of Minucius Felix,* Ch. 10

early church writers. Why do some people today still try to mold God into their own image?

SUMMARY

Our modern churches have done an outstanding job of obscuring the simple plan of salvation that was given in the New Testament, practiced in the New Testament, and witnessed by the early church writers. Let us resolve to return to His Church and His plan of salvation. Let us, as His servants, use Biblical terms in describing the Plan and in describing those who have followed His Plan. In this way, we can more effectively submit to Him as Lord and Master.

Chapter 10

MARRIAGE IN CHRIST'S CHURCH

INTRODUCTION

It is said that the family is the foundation of society. It is also a fundamental building block of His Church. Marriage was instituted by God in the Old Testament and blessed by Christ Himself. As Christians, we need to honor and respect this most important bond in Christ's Church. In this chapter, we shall examine marriage and divorce as written in both the Bible and in the writings of the early church fathers.

MARRIAGE

Christ blessed marriage during His first miracle. It is within the safety of marriage that children are to be nurtured and grow into His Children. However, today, marriage is being assaulted from every side. Men are being accepted as unnecessary in a child's life, women are being used as playthings and then thrown away, and homosexuals are seeking "marriage." What does God have to say?

In the Old Testament, marriage outside of the Hebrew nation was an intolerable sin. In Ezra, those who had married foreign wives were required to divorce them, for they had disobeyed God, *"You have been unfaithful and have married foreign wives adding to the guilt of Israel."* EZRA 10:10. In addition, priests were restricted as to whom they could marry, *"They shall not take a woman who is profaned by harlotry, nor shall they take a woman divorced from her husband; "* LEV. 21:7. Thus, God is particular about our marriages. We need to heed His advice.

Christ blessed marriage by performing His first miracle at the wedding in Cana of Galilee, where He turned the water into wine, John 2:1. The writer of Hebrews also esteems marriage, *"Let marriage be held in honor among all, and let the marriage bed be undefiled; for fornicators and adulterers God will judge."* HEB. 13:4. The Shepherd of Hermas (140 AD) also blesses marriage, *"And I said, 'If a wife or husband die, and the widower or widow marry, does he or she commit sin?' 'There is no sin in marrying again,' said he; 'but if they remain unmarried, they gain greater honour and glory with the Lord; but if they marry, they do not sin. Guard, therefore, your chastity and purity, and you will live to God.'"* [105] Note that the emphasis of both the Hebrews passage and the Shepherd passage is on remaining undefiled. We should seek to be pure priests of God.

Irenaeus (185 AD) criticizes Saturninus and Basilides for disparaging marriage, *"They declare also, that marriage and generation are from Satan."* [106] He goes on, *"Springing from Saturninus and Marcion, those who are called Encratites (self-controlled) preached against marriage, thus setting aside the original creation of God, and indirectly blaming Him who made the male and female for the propagation of the human race."* [107] Thus, he sanctions marriage as from God.

Ignatius (106 AD) advises couples to seek the approval of the bishop, *"But it becomes both men and women who marry, to form their union with the approval of the bishop, that their marriage may be according to God, and not after their own lust."* [108] Keep in mind he believed in one bishop and multiple elders. We should interpret his remarks as asking couples to obtain the approval of the elders. Isn't this a great idea?

We should note here that chastity was not a virtue universally practiced. There were those willing to tear apart

---

[105] *Shepherd of Hermas, Commandment Fourth,* Ch. 4
[106] Irenaeus, *Against Heresies,* Book 1, Ch. 24:2
[107] Irenaeus, *Against Heresies,* Book 1, Ch. 28:1
[108] Ignatius, *Epistle to Polycarp,* Ch. 5

marriages in that day the same as in our day Theophilus (170 AD) writes, *"And Epicurus himself, too, as well as teaching atheism, teaches along with it incest with mothers and sisters, and this in transgression of the laws which forbid it; for Solon distinctly legislated regarding this, in order that from a married parent children might lawfully spring, that they might not be born of adultery, so that no one should honour as his father him who was not his father, or dishonour him who was really his father, through ignorance that he was so. And these things the other laws of the Romans and Greeks also prohibit. Why, then, do Epicurus and the Stoics teach incest and sodomy, with which doctrines they have filled libraries, so that from boyhood this lawless intercourse is learned? And why should I further spend time on them, since even of those they call gods they relate similar things?"* [109] Note that those teaching these things were filling the libraries with this immoral philosophy. Do you see any similarities with today's society?

Justin (150 AD), in his defense of Christianity to the Emperor, *"But whether we marry, it is only that we may bring up children; or whether we decline marriage, we live continently. And that you may understand that promiscuous intercourse is not one of our mysteries,"* [110] He was telling the emperor that Christians are not promiscuous, that they can live contentedly both in marriage, and single. Can we justify Justin's confidence in us, today?

DIVORCE

This is, for me, one of the most difficult subjects about which to write. I know personally of Christians who have gone through divorce and am keenly aware of the pain it causes the divorcees and their families. I also have to admit, at this point, that I do not know everything. My knowledge of God is still

---

[109] Theophilus, *Letter to Autolycus,* Book 3, Ch. 6
[110] Justin, *First Apology,* Ch. 29

growing, and is, therefore, imperfect. However, I must be honest with the readers. Therefore, I will, within this section, try my best to present the complete Biblical view and the views of those great men who followed the apostolic age. If you find my discussion incomplete, then I ask, in advance, for your forgiveness.

Tertullian (207 AD) lamented that divorce had become so common in society, *"Where is that happiness of married life, ever so desirable, which distinguished our earlier manners, and as the result of which for about 600 years there was not among us a single divorce? Now, women have every member of the body heavy laden with gold; wine-bibbing is so common among them, that the kiss is never offered with their will; and as for divorce, they long for it as though it were the natural consequence of marriage."* [111] Does this sound similar to our society today? Divorce has become a common, yet painful experience in many lives today — both within the church and without the church. We, as His Church, need a clear understanding of divorce so we can be compassionate servants of Him.

God makes His position on divorce quite clear in Malachi, where He declares, *"For I hate divorce."* MAL. 2:16A. He meant married couples to stay married. In Genesis, He says, *"For this cause a man shall leave his father and his mother, and shall cleave to his wife; and they shall become one flesh."* GEN. 2:24. This was His plan for us — His plan for His people. This ought to be the goal of every one of us who carries His name.

However, man caused God's plan to go awry. Therefore, under the Old Testament law, divorce could be initiated by the husband. The first mention of divorce is in the Bible is, *"When a man takes a wife and marries her, and it happens that she finds no favor in his eyes because he has found*

---

[111] Tertullian, *The Apology,* Ch. 6

some indecency in her, and he writes her a certificate of divorce and puts it in her hand and sends her out from his house," DEUT. 24:1. There was disagreement among the Jews about what the indecency could be. The stricter Jews accepted only adultery as grounds for divorce, whereas the more liberal Jews accepted any reason.

In the New Testament, Jesus is asked a direct question about divorce. *"And some Pharisees came to Him, testing Him, and saying, 'Is it lawful for a man to divorce his wife for any cause at all?' And He answered and said, 'Have you not read, that He who created them from the beginning made them male and female,' and said, 'For this cause a man shall leave his father and mother, and shall cleave to his wife; and the two shall become one flesh?' 'Consequently they are no longer two, but one flesh. What therefore God has joined together, let no man separate.' They *said to Him, 'Why then did Moses command to give her a certificate of divorce and send her away?' He *said to them, 'Because of your hardness of heart, Moses permitted you to divorce your wives; but from the beginning it has not been this way. And I say to you, whoever divorces his wife, except for immorality, and marries another woman commits adultery.'"* MATT. 19:3-9.

The reason the Pharisees asked the question was to see which side Jesus came down on — the liberal side, permitting any reason for divorce, or the conservative side, permitting only adultery. His answer stated Gods plan — God does not want any to divorce.

Remarriage After Divorce

Reread the passage more closely. Note that Jesus is saying that if divorce and remarriage occur, then adultery occurs (except for immorality). However, Mark provides us more guidance, *"And He *said to them, 'Whoever divorces his wife and marries another woman commits adultery against her;*

and if she herself divorces her husband and marries another man, she is committing adultery.'" MARK 10:11-12. Thus, if the wife divorces and remarries, then she commits adultery (presumably even if she had, thus far, been faithful to her husband). We must conclude from this passage that the sin of adultery occurs when remarriage occurs.

Luke makes the case even clearer when he states, *"and he who marries one who is divorced from a husband commits adultery."* LUKE 16:18. Thus, not only is the divorcing party committing adultery by remarriage, but the party to which the divorcing party is joined is also committing adultery.

Why is this? Marriage is a contract between a man and a woman. If one of them breaks the contract via adultery, then the contract can no longer endure. If one of them divorces for unlawful reasons, and then remarries, the first contract is broken, and adultery occurs. Thus, Jesus has carefully outlined two conditions for adultery:

(1) Infidelity in the first marriage
(2) Remarriage from an unlawful divorce.

God's goal for our lives is that we solve our problems and remain together.

Divorce from an Unbeliever

When the Jews had returned from Babylon, Ezra found out that many of them had taken foreign wives, contrary to the law. Therefore, Ezra instructed them to divorce their foreign wives, to which they responded, *"And they pledged to put away their wives, and being guilty, they offered a ram of the flock for their offense."* EZRA 10:19.

Paul was afraid that the early Christians would follow this example. That is, if they had married prior to becoming a Christian, their coming to Christ could serve as an excuse for getting out of the marriage. Paul then addressed the matter in 1 Corinthians. He first addressed those couples who were both Christians, *"But to the married I give instructions, not I, but the Lord, that the wife should not leave her husband (but if she does leave, let her remain unmarried, or else be reconciled to her husband), and that the husband should not send his wife away."* 1 COR. 7:10-11.   Here, Paul indicates that he heard this directly from the Lord. A divorce should not occur. However, if it does, the wife (and presumably the husband) should remain unmarried so that reconciliation could occur.

Next, Paul, not having received any instructions from Christ, addresses Christians with an unbelieving spouse. *"But to the rest I say, not the Lord, that if any brother has a wife who is an unbeliever, and she consents to live with him, let him not send her away. And a woman who has an unbelieving husband, and he consents to live with her, let her not send her husband away."* 1 COR. 7:12-14. Thus, Christians are NOT to do as Ezra's people did, but are to remain with their spouses.

But what if the unbelieving spouse insists upon leaving? Paul writes, *"Yet if the unbelieving one leaves, let him leave; the brother or the sister is not under bondage in such cases, but God has called us to peace."* 1 COR. 7:15. Thus, a Christian may not seek a divorce, but he may accept one if the unbelieving spouse insists on it.

Is such a divorced Christian then free to remarry? There are those who interpret "under bondage" as meaning "under the marriage contract." Thus, they would permit remarriage, for the contract is no longer valid. However, the word used here is the Greek word, douloō (δούλοω). This is the common word for "being enslaved."   It is used eight times in the New Testament[112] indicating such things as being enslaved to Babylon, to sin, to God, to righteousness, and to the world. In

---

[112] ACTS 7:6, ROM. 6:18, ROM. 6:22, 1 COR. 7:15, 1 COR. 9:19, GAL. 4:3, TIT. 2:3, and 2 PET. 2:19.

addition, over 50 times, forms of this word are used to express slavery, serving, bondage, and similar thoughts.   However, never is it used in the New Testament to represent a contract, and never is it used to represent the contract of marriage. Thus, it appears that, here, Paul is trying to express that, for the Christian to remain where he/she is neither loved nor wanted would be tantamount to slavery. In these cases, chaos would result, and peace within the marriage would be destroyed and, he notes, we were called to peace. Thus, separation is justified.

In such a case, could the injured party divorce and remarry? Paul answers this in expressing what the ultimate outcome of such a case could be, *"For how do you know, O wife, whether you will save your husband? Or how do you know, O husband, whether you will save your wife?"* 1 COR. 7:16. It is clear that Paul wants reconciliation, not permanent separation. Anything (including remarriage) that prevented that reconciliation from occurring should be avoided.

Early Writers Discuss Divorce and Remarriage
The following passage from Shepherd of Hermas (140 AD) gives an excellent description of divorce as viewed by early writers, *"'Sir, if any one has a wife who trusts in the Lord, and if he detect her in adultery, does the man sin if he continue to live with her?' And he said to me, 'As long as he remains ignorant of her sin, the husband commits no transgression in living with her. But if the husband know that his wife has gone astray, and if the woman does not repent, but persists in her fornication, and yet the husband continues to live with her, he also is guilty of her crime, and a sharer in her adultery.' And I said to him, 'What then, sir, is the husband to do, if his wife continue in her vicious practices?' And he said, 'The husband should put her away, and remain by himself. But if he put his wife away and marry another, he also commits adultery.' And I said to him, 'What if the woman put away should repent, and*

wish to return to her husband: shall she not be taken back by her husband?' And he said to me, 'Assuredly. If the husband do not take her back, he sins, and brings a great sin upon himself; for he ought to take back the sinner who has repented. But not frequently.'" [113]

There are a number of lessons in this passage. First, if a spouse is involved in adultery, it is viewed as so great a breach of the marriage covenant that it cannot be tolerated by the other spouse. Second, it is grounds for divorce. Third, however, the aggrieved party is to remain single. That way, if the aggrieving party repents, the breach can be healed and God's plan for marriage put back on track.

Justin Martyr (150 AD) echoes the view that the remarriage is the sin, *"And, 'Whosoever shall marry her that is divorced from another husband, committeth adultery.' ... So that all who, by human law, are twice married, are in the eye of our Master sinners, ..."* [114] Theophylis (170 AD), also, restates the sin of remarrying, *"'Whosoever looketh on a woman who is not his own wife, to lust after her, hath committed adultery with her already in his heart.' 'And he that marrieth,' says [the Gospel], 'her that is divorced from her husband, committeth adultery; and whosoever putteth away his wife, saving for the cause of fornication, causeth her to commit adultery.'"* [115] Notice that he, too, permits adultery as a grounds for divorce.

Tertullian (207 AD) takes the position that Moses allowed divorce and Christ prohibited it. *"But Christ prohibits divorce, saying, 'Whosoever putteth away his wife, and marrieth another, committeth adultery; and whosoever marrieth her that is put away from her husband, also committeth adultery.' In order to forbid divorce, He makes it unlawful to marry a woman*

---

[113] *Shepherd of Hermas, Commandment Fourth*, Ch. 1. Note that this last case assumes that neither spouse has remarried. Deut. 24:1-4 would prohibit reconciliation if remarriage had occurred.

[114] Justin Martyr, *First Apology*, Ch. 15

[115] *Theophilus to Autolycus*, Book 3, Ch. 13

that has been put away. Moses, however, permitted repudiation in Deuteronomy: ... " [116] However, he goes on to say that Christ sanctioned the provisions of Moses because of the hardness of their hearts. Tertullian writes further that the goal of Christ's teaching was to maintain the bond of marriage intact, *"Even Christ, however, when He here commands 'the wife not to depart from her husband, or if she depart, to remain unmarried or be reconciled to her husband,' both permitted divorce, which indeed He never absolutely prohibited, and confirmed (the sanctity) of marriage, by first forbidding its dissolution; and, if separation had taken place, by wishing the nuptial bond to be resumed by reconciliation."* [117]

What do we learn from this? The Bible and early church writers who read the Bible permitted divorce for only one reason — adultery. However, none of them permitted the divorced persons to remarry without incurring the sin of adultery. It was and is God's plan to maintain the marriage bond.

When Reconciliation is Impossible

What shall we say when a divorce has occurred, and one of the partners is irreconcilable or remarries? Is the other partner free to remarry? In this book, I have tried to present the views of both the Bible and the Early Writings. However, I know of no way to answer this particular question. Thus, it would seem that each person who finds himself/herself in this situation should carefully study the Bible and the early writings cited above, and prayerfully make the best decision he/she can make. The rest of us, as loving brothers and sisters, should then support these decisions, recognizing the agony our brothers have endured and the dedication they have to our common Savior.

---

[116] Tertullian, *Against Marcion,* Book 4, Ch. 34
[117] Tertullian, *Against Marcion,* Book 5, Ch. 7

Is Divorce a Sin and, if so, Unforgivable?

Next we have to ask the question, "Is divorce a sin?" Obviously, it is not God's intention that divorce occur. Any time a divorce occurs, it is a frustration of God's will for two lives. However, because we are mortal, because we are imperfect, divorce does occur. Whether it is a sin or not is dependent upon the circumstances. Furthermore, it is not for me to judge whether another sins or not. God is the Father, not I.

If divorce occurs, and it was a sin, is that sin an unforgivable sin? Of course it is not. However, many churches treat it as unforgivable. It is a sin that Jesus can forgive, just as He can forgive the sins of lying, stealing, and infidelity. If He forgave Paul's killing of Christians, certainly He can forgive a sinful divorce. We, as Christians, need to emulate His forgiveness. Besides, if sin was involved, that sin is not against us, it is against Him and the two parties involved.

Is the remarriage a sin? Again, it is not for us to judge. This is God's domain. Whatever happens, we need to treat all sinners as we treat ourselves, for we are, also, sinners in need of His grace.

A PRESCRIPTION FOR MARRIAGES IN TROUBLE

The Bible tells us that the man is the head of the woman, *"But I want you to understand that Christ is the head of every man, and the man is the head of a woman, and God is the head of Christ."* 1 COR. 11:3. The man is also the head of the marriage in the same way that Christ is Head of His Church, *"Wives, be subject to your own husbands, as to the Lord. For the husband is the head of the wife, as Christ also is the head of the church, He Himself being the Savior of the body."* EPH. 5:22-23. Thus, if the marriage is in trouble, it is the man who has the obligation to see to it that things are set right. This means that it is the husband who has the obligation to seek out advice and counsel — not the wife. Thus, as a first step in solving the divorce problem, we in His Church need to teach husbands that their obligations to marriage include keeping the bond intact. We need to impress on new husbands that they have the obligation to seek help when problems occur that the two of them cannot handle. They should not enter into marriage unless they have this understanding of their obligation to each other and to Christ.

Over twenty years ago, a young lady came to me and wanted me to teach her new boyfriend about Christ. We met together and studied and, ultimately, I baptized him into Christ. We watched them marry, have children, and lead lives within the Church. Recently, however, I learned that he and she were having some marriage difficulties, so I called him to see if we could meet. I wanted to speak to him about counseling, to see if they could patch things up. However, he never found the time to meet with me. Now, they are divorced. What a tragedy! It leaves a great hole in my heart to know that they will not enjoy the pleasures of marriage in their old age, and to see the pain that the divorce has caused. Divorce affects everyone around us. Men need to step up to the plate and assume their role as leader and "fix what needs fix'n." If that means counseling by a third party, get it! If that means changing, do it!

Second, since His Church has pastors, each new husband needs to be pastored by a person who can help them along the way. The present buzz term is mentoring. We need pastors who can mentor to young marriages to help them see how to solve problems along the way. This needs to continue for an extended period of time.

Because many churches have adopted the "our church" approach, and have appointed one pastor, they cannot do this. The single pastor would be totally overworked. In addition, when premarital counseling is provided, the "pastor" provides it. Further down the line, when the marriage encounters problems, the "pastor" has moved on to another congregation and the couple is older and does not want to have a young, inexperienced "pastor" try to counsel them in their marriage. However, if we follow His Plan, and have multiple pastors as He says, and actually do the shepherding He wants us to do, we can accomplish His will in this phase of the church, too.

Both of these suggestions require an understanding that marriage is not just an obligation to each other. It is an obligation we take to the children produced by that marriage and to everyone affected by divorce. Most important of all, it is an obligation that we take to Christ and His Church.

CONCLUSION

As His Church, we need to honor the institutions He honored. Today, our marriages in the church are in trouble, for we are adopting the world's view, instead of His View. We need to work as individuals and as a church to make marriages within the church what He wants them to be

Chapter 11

OTHER DOCTRINES OF CHRIST'S CHURCH

INTRODUCTION

We have many ethical and doctrinal issues in our present society that were addressed by the early church writers. We shall examine some of them in this chapter.

MIRACULOUS GIFTS OF THE HOLY SPIRIT

There are many churches today that assert that the miraculous gifts of the Holy Spirit are at work today; that there are people who have miraculous healing powers, miraculous gifts of prophecy, and speak in languages that they were not taught (that is, speak in tongues). Let us first examine what the Bible says about this.

The miraculous gifts were bestowed on the day of Pentecost. Luke writes in Acts, *"And when the day of Pentecost had come, they were all together in one place. And suddenly there came from heaven a noise like a violent, rushing wind, and it filled the whole house where they were sitting. And there appeared to them tongues as of fire distributing themselves, and they rested on each one of them. And they were all filled with the Holy Spirit and began to speak with other tongues, as the Spirit was giving them utterance."* ACTS 2:1-4. Thus, there is no doubt that miraculous gifts were given. But to whom were they given? The "they" in the first sentence refers to whatever group preceded the "they" in the passage. If we look at the last verse of Chapter 1, the passage clearly identifies "they" as the apostles, *"And they drew lots for them, and the lot fell to Matthias; and he was numbered with the eleven apostles."* ACTS 1:26. Keep in mind that the original text of the New Testament was in Greek, without verse divisions or chapter divisions.

The Word confirms this in Acts chapter eight. In verse five, we are told that Philip preached to the people of Samaria, resulting in the conversion of many to Christ. In verse nine, we are introduced to Simon, a former magician who was converted to Christ. Philip had great success in his ministry, *"But when they believed Philip preaching the good news about the kingdom of God and the name of Jesus Christ, they were being baptized, men and women alike. And even Simon himself believed; and after being baptized, he continued on with Philip; and as he observed signs and great miracles taking place, he was constantly amazed."* ACTS 8:12-13. The scripture then records, *"Now when the apostles in Jerusalem heard that Samaria had received the word of God, they sent them Peter and John, who came down and prayed for them, that they might receive the Holy Spirit."* ACTS 8:14-15. Why had these people not received the miraculous gifts of the Holy Spirit directly from Philip, since he obviously possessed these gifts? He was there and he changed peoples lives. The answer to this question comes in the succeeding verses, *"Then they began laying their hands on them, and they were receiving the Holy Spirit. Now when Simon saw that the Spirit was bestowed through the laying on of the apostles' hands, he offered them money, saying, 'Give this authority to me as well, so that everyone on whom I lay my hands may receive the Holy Spirit.'"* ACTS 8:18-19. Simon knew that the gifts were given "through the laying on of apostles' hands." Thus, Philip, even though he had the gift, could not give it to others — only the apostles could give the gift. From the Bible text, we can only conclude that (a) the apostles, and only the apostles, received the entire, miraculous gifts of the Holy Spirit, and (b) they had the ability to pass these on to whom they chose, but (c) those persons receiving gifts from the apostles did not have the ability to pass on the gifts to others.

Paul corroborates this scenario in 1 Corinthians, *"Love never fails; but if there are gifts of prophecy, they will be done away; if there are tongues, they will cease; if there is knowledge, it will be done away."* 1 COR. 13:8. Tongues would cease; prophecy would cease; miraculous knowledge would cease. In fact, it did cease when those who received these gifts from the apostles died.

The writings of the early church authors substantiate this. There are very few references to the miraculous gifts, because all of these writers knew that the gifts had ceased. The gifts were not a problem as they were to Paul, because the gifts were no longer active. There is no writing telling us to obtain these gifts or instructing us to use these gifts. They all recognized that God had given these gifts to the apostles and given partial gifts to their successors.

Clement of Alexandria (200 AD), quoting 1 Cor. 12:7-11, declares that the apostles had the perfections in miraculous gifts, *"The manifestation of the Spirit is given for our profit. For to one is given the word of wisdom by the Spirit; to another the word of knowledge according to the same Spirit; to another faith through the same Spirit; to another the gifts of healing through the same Spirit; to another the working of miracles; to another prophecy; to another discernment of spirits; to another diversities of tongues; to another the interpretation of tongues: and all these worketh the one and the same Spirit, distributing to each one according as He wills.' Such being the case, the prophets are perfect in prophecy, the righteous in righteousness, and the martyrs in confession, and others in preaching, not that they are not sharers in the common virtues, but are proficient in those to which they are appointed."* [118]

---

[118] Clement of Alexandria, *The Stromata or Miscellanies*, Book 4, Ch. 21

Tertullian (207 AD) asserts that the miraculous gifts were given to the apostles only, *"'He gave gifts to the sons of men,' that is, the gratuities, which we call charismata. He says specifically 'sons of men,' and not men promiscuously; thus exhibiting to us those who were the children of men truly so called, choice men, apostles."* [119] Note that he restricts the gifts to the apostles. In one of his other writings, Tertullian testifies that the apostles had the full gifts of the Holy Spirit, and that we have the Holy Spirit partially, *"For apostles have the Holy Spirit properly, who have Him fully, in the operations of prophecy, and the efficacy of (healing) virtues, and the evidences of tongues; not partially, as all others have."* [120] Here he identifies prophecy, healing, and tongues as full measures of the Holy Spirit and clearly states that we do not have this full measure.

I have had personal experience with those who claim to have the gift. When I was a boy, I had an affliction that we wanted healed. My grandmother took me to one of these "miraculous healers" and he prayed for my healing. It did not occur. He failed. Christ never failed. The apostle Paul never failed. Christ's name is not uplifted by failure. I have reached the conclusion that if a person has even one failure at healing, this is one too many. Christ never fails.

When I was young, I had the experience of observing my grandmother "speak in tongues" during one of the church services. I shall quote her directly, *"tut, tut, tut, tut."* She was not speaking in an organized language. She was speaking an ecstatic utterance, as one lover would speak to another in the throes of passion. The tongues of the New Testament were organized languages, understood by many. I admire my grandmother for loving Christ so much, but I cannot accept her love-speak as being of the same type and class as that in Acts 2.

---

[119] Tertullian, *Against Marcion*, Book 5, Ch. 8
[120] Tertullian, *Exhortation to Chastity*, Book 5, Ch. 4

Thus, the Bible, the early church writers, and my own experience tell me that we cannot and do not receive the miraculous gifts of the Holy Spirit today. This is not to say that God does not work miracles. I believe that He can and does work miracles in our lives as He chooses. However, it is as He chooses and as He wills.

ABORTION

Abortion has been an issue that has divided the United States politically. The Bible mentions the consequences of causing an abortion during a fight, *"And if men struggle with each other and strike a woman with child so that she has a miscarriage, yet there is no further injury, he shall surely be fined as the woman's husband may demand of him; and he shall pay as the judges decide."* EX. 21:22. Thus, the unborn child was considered of value. Paul speaks of himself being untimely born, (Greek, ektrōma, ἔκτρωμα), meaning a miscarriage, one born immature or incompletely formed.

What do the early church writers say of abortion? The Epistle of Barnabus (75 AD) says, *"Thou shalt not slay the child by procuring abortion; nor, again, shalt thou destroy it after it is born."*[121] Thus, they considered it murder. The Didache (120 AD) is very clear on the issue, *"thou shalt not murder a child by abortion nor kill that which is begotten."*[122] Apostolic Constitutions (350 AD) echoes the Didache, *"Thou shall not slay thy child by causing abortion, nor kill that which is begotten; for 'everything that is shaped, and has received a soul from God, if it be slain, shall be avenged, as being unjustly destroyed.'"*[123]

Athenagoras (177 AD) condemns murder in gladiator games and abortion in the same passage, *"How, then, when we*

---

[121] *Epistle of Barnabus,* Ch. 19
[122] *Didache,* Ch. 2:2
[123] *Apostolic Constitutions,* Book 7, Ch. 3

do not even look on [gladiator games with wild beasts], *lest we should contract guilt and pollution, can we put people to death? And when we say that those women who use drugs to bring on abortion commit murder, and will have to give an account to God for the abortion, on what principle should we commit murder? For it does not belong to the same person to regard the very foetus in the womb as a created being, and therefore an object of God's care, and when it has passed into life, to kill it; and not to expose an infant, because those who expose them are chargeable with child-murder, and on the other hand, when it has been reared to destroy it.*" [124]

Tertullian (207 AD) expresses the view that the unborn child is the start of a human, *"The embryo therefore becomes a human being in the womb from the moment that its form is completed. The law of Moses, indeed, punishes with due penalties the man who shall cause abortion, inasmuch as there exists already the rudiment of a human being."* [125] Thus, to him, abortion was considered the taking of a human life, and, therefore, punishable.

Minucius Felix, (190 AD) a contemporary with Tertullian, criticizes abortion in the following passage: *"There are some women who, by drinking medical preparations, extinguish the source of the future man in their very bowels, and thus commit a parricide before they bring forth."*[126] Hippolytus (220 AD), a disciple of Irenaeus, condemns trying to produce an abortion, *"Whence women, reputed believers, began to resort to drugs for producing sterility, and to gird themselves round, so to expel what was being conceived on account of their not wishing to have a child either by a slave or by any paltry fellow, for the sake of their family and excessive wealth. Behold, into how*

[124] Athenagoras, *A Plea for the Christians,* Ch. 35.
[125] Tertullian, *A Treatise on the Soul,* Ch. 37
[126] Minucius Felix, *The Octavius of Minucius Felix,* Ch. 30

great impiety that lawless one has proceeded, by inculcating adultery and murder at the same time!" [127]

Finally, a spurious book from 175-200 AD, the Revelation of Peter, sees in a vision, *"And near that place I saw another strait place into which the gore and the filth of those who were being punished ran down and became there as it were a lake: and there sat women having the gore up to their necks, and over against them sat many children who were born to them out of due time, crying; and there came forth from them sparks of fire and smote the women in the eyes: and these were the accursed who conceived and caused abortion."* [128]

What can we draw from all of these references? The opposition to abortion in the early church was well documented. It was considered the murder of a child by these writers.

HOMOSEXUALITY

Homosexuality has become one of the hot topics of the 20th and 21st centuries. However, before we tackle homosexuality, let us look at some of the moral issues facing the heterosexual person. We can divide the problem into two issues. The first issue is one of the desires of a person. Is it a sin to have sexual desires when you are not married? Obviously not. Paul addresses the unmarried, *" But I say to the unmarried and to widows that it is good for them if they remain even as I. But if they do not have self-control, let them marry; for it is better to marry than to burn."* 1 COR. 7:8-9. He assumes that the unmarried have sexual desires. The only question is whether the person has self-control. Thus, such desires are part of the natural person.

---

[127] Hippolytus, *The Refutation of All Heresies,* Book 9, Ch. 7

[128] *Revelation of Peter,* vs 25. This was not written by the apostle; we do not know its author. It dates from the third quarter of the second century. It does, however, give us an opinion of abortion from a person of that early date.

The second issue concerns the behavior. Is the behavior of having sex outside marriage condemned? The Book of Hebrews advises, *"Let marriage be held in honor among all, and let the marriage bed be undefiled; for fornicators and adulterers God will judge."* HEB. 13:4. The writer expects chaste behavior of us. Regardless of his/her desires, it is expected that these desires be kept within the bonds of marriage.

Thus, there is a difference between the desires of a person and the behavior of a person. We can use this same logic in the analysis of homosexuality. We can separate this issue into these same two different questions. The first is the question of the homosexual person. Is the person automatically a sinner because the person has homosexual desires? The second is the behavior itself. Are homosexual acts condemned?

Let us examine the bodies of male and female. Obviously, the intent of the creator of these bodies was that these two bodies are made for each other; the male is made for the female and the female is made for the male. In addition the only way that offspring can be conceived involves a male and a female. Thus, God, the creator of these two bodies, obviously intended that these two sexes formed the basis for a family into which a child could be born. Our very creation screams heterosexuality.

But is homosexuality wrong? The Bible gives us instruction on this subject. Leviticus tells us, *"You shall not lie with a male as one lies with a female; it is an abomination."* LEV. 18:22. Here, male homosexual *behavior* is condemned and, in Lev. 20:13, he prescribes death as the penalty for such behavior. Note that the *behavior* is condemned, not the desires of the person. In Jude it is written, *"Just as Sodom and Gomorrah and the cities around them, since they in the same way as these indulged in gross immorality and went after strange flesh, are exhibited as an example, in undergoing the punishment of eternal fire."* JUDE 7. The "strange flesh" was, in general, going after flesh that God had not intended and, specifically, going after the angels. Thus, there is flesh that is outside of God's law. But it is the *behavior* that is condemned. They *indulged* in gross immorality; they *went* after strange flesh.

Paul roundly condemns the actions of homosexuality in Romans, *"For this reason God gave them over to degrading passions; for their women exchanged the natural function for that which is unnatural, and in the same way also the men abandoned the natural function of the woman and burned in their desire toward one another, men with men committing indecent acts and receiving in their own persons the due penalty of their error."* ROM. 1:26-27. Here, it is very difficult to miss his meaning. He calls male with male intercourse "indecent acts". The "in the same way" indicates that the "unnatural" [literally, "against nature"] acts that the women were engaging in were the same as described for the men, namely, homosexual acts. Note that he condemns the *behavior* and he also condemns them for giving in to their passions.

It should also be noted that homosexuality is included in the two lists of sins, one in 1 Cor. 6:9, and the other in 1 Tim. 1:10. In both of these cases, the Greek word used is arsenokoitēs (ἀρσενοκοίτης) from arseno, (a male), and koitēs, (a place to lie or a place to conceive — we get "coitus" from this). The word "koitēs" is used elsewhere where it refers to the marriage bed, Thus, arsenokoitēs means to lie with a male as with a female. It definitely refers to male homosexuality. Here, it is the *behavior* that is specifically forbidden.

Tertullian (207 AD) suggests that there is unnatural sin with man, *"and who threatened with death the unchaste, sacrilegious, and monstrous abomination both of adultery and unnatural sin with man and beast."* [129] It is reasonable to

---

[129] Tertullian, *Against Marcion,* Book 1, Ch. 29

assume he meant homosexuality. Again, the *behavior* is condemned. Apostolic Constitutions (350 AD) condemns both homosexuality and adultery as follows, *"For the sin of Sodom is contrary to nature, as is also that with brute beasts. But adultery and fornication are against the law; the one whereof is impiety, the other injustice, and, in a word, no other than a great sin. But neither sort of them is without its punishment in its own proper nature. For the practisers of one sort attempt the dissolution of the world, and endeavour to make the natural course of things to change for one that is unnatural; but those of the second son—the adulterers—are unjust by corrupting others' marriages, and dividing into two what God hath made one, rendering the children suspected, and exposing the true husband to the snares of others. And fornication is the destruction of one's own flesh, not being made use of for the procreation of children, but entirely for the sake of pleasure, which is a mark of incontinency, and not a sign of virtue. All these things are forbidden by the laws; for thus say the oracles: 'Thou shalt not lie with mankind as with womankind.' 'For such a one is accursed, and ye shall stone them with stones: they have wrought abomination.'"* [130] It is clear that homosexual *behavior* is condemned.

Polycarp (110 AD), also, warns against homosexuality, especially in young men, *"In like manner, let the young men also be blameless in all things, being especially careful to preserve purity, and keeping themselves in, as with a bridle, from every kind of evil. For it is well that they should be cut off from the lusts that are in the world, since 'every lust warreth against the spirit;' and 'neither fornicators, nor effeminate, nor abusers of themselves with mankind, shall inherit the kingdom of God,' nor those who do things inconsistent and unbecoming. Wherefore, it is needful to abstain from all these things, ..."*[131]

---

[130] *Apostolic Constitutions,* Book 6, ch. 28
[131] Polycarp, *Epistle to the Philippians,* Ch. 5

It seems an inescapable conclusion that the *behavior* of homosexuality is condemned, both by the Bible and by the post-apostolic writers. They acknowledge that each of us have sexual desires. However, God expects us to keep our passions in check, whether homosexual or heterosexual, reserving sexual relations for a marriage consisting of a male and a female. He expects this of the 16-year-old girl in high school, He expects this of the 24-year-old single man, and He expects of the 64-year old widow. It make no difference to Him whether the desires of man are for the opposite sex, the same sex, or for robbing a bank. In each case, He expects us to keep these desires in check — to be moral persons. Clement of Alexandria (200 AD) cautions that passion can be the root of sin. Therefore, he admonishes us to cut out the lust, which is the root of inordinate passion, *"For He is admirable always at cutting out the roots of sins, such as, 'Thou shalt not commit adultery,' by 'Thou shalt not lust.'"* [132] Sexual relations are reserved exclusively for those between a husband and his wife. We need to focus ourselves on this fact. We cannot escape this responsibility to ourselves, to His Church, and to our Lord God.

---

[132] Clement of Alexandria, *The Instructor*, Book 2, Ch. 6

Chapter 12

BUILDING CHRIST'S CHURCH TODAY

INTRODUCTION

In today's atmosphere of denominationalism, with numerous extra-Biblical doctrines swirling throughout Christendom, is it even *possible* to build His Church today? Can we go back to His pattern for His Church? The answer to these questions is a resounding "yes." He is still Master of His Church and, if we let Him, He can still be Master of our lives.

THE FOUNDATION

The foundation for His Church starts with each of us, as individuals, building on that foundation. The most fundamental part of this foundation is the bedrock that under girds the foundation. This bedrock was stated by Peter when he declared, *"Thou art the Christ, the Son of the Living God."* MATT. 16:16.

He is, first of all, the *Christ*. It was He that was pointed out in the Old Testament. His people have sought Him all of their existence and, now, He is here and we rejoice for His being here.

Peter confessed that He is also the *Son*. Through Him, and only through Him, we can seek out the Father, to determine the Father's will for our lives. It is through His marvelous salvation that we can have access to the Father. It is He that permits us to live free from the burden of sin, allowing us to blossom, to expand our horizons, and to become all that we can be in Him.

Peter also declared that He is *living*. That is, He permeates our beings; His will is constantly being sought and

144

followed by us. He is dynamic, a force within our lives that causes us to be successful in anything we do. Paul says, *"I can do all things through Him who strengthens me."* PHIL. 4:13. By this he means that he can live in poverty, he can live in plenty, he can live in any circumstance that faces him. How can we be anything but successful with this kind of attitude, with this kind of Force, in our lives? Success — the kind defined by God — is ours when we submit our lives to Christ.

Jesus is also *God in His fullness*. As such, He has power over the universe, over sin, and over us. We can tap into that power by turning our complete lives over to Him so He can mold us to be the kind of person He wants. His power permits us to succeed, to endure pain, and to enjoy life to the fullest. His power floods our lives with light and with strength so that we can overcome the obstacles that this life and that Satan throw in our way. What confidence this gives us!

Not only is Jesus God, but He has permitted us to have direct access to Him and His power through prayer and through participation in His Church. He works along side us as we go to work, as we play, as we go through the hard times of life; encouraging us in everything we do. This personal relationship provides the underpinnings for our lives, making us the successes that we are.

But where do we encounter Christ? Paul zealously encourages us, *"So then you are no longer strangers and aliens, but you are fellow citizens with the saints, and are of God's household, having been built upon the foundation of the apostles and prophets, Christ Jesus Himself being the corner stone, in whom the whole building, being fitted together is growing into a holy temple in the Lord;"* EPH. 2:19-21. Through His Word, we get to know Him, to know what He has for our lives. Through this marvelous encounter, we are able to more fully understand what part He has in our goals and aspirations. What does this mean to us? Each Christian must search out the scriptures to determine Christ's pattern for his life. We need to study diligently to perceive His thoughts as they are revealed through His Holy Word and to thoughtfully pray that these words will become real in our souls. This means we have to study, study, study. This is an active process, requiring our attention to reading, to prayer, and to discipleship. We need to carry the hearing over to the doing.

Once we, as members, have built on the apostles and prophets, Christ being the Chief Corner Stone, we can, collectively build His Church. Note that building His Church requires committed Christians, those who eagerly seek His leading in their lives. His Church is not built in seminaries, but in the hearts of individuals who come to know Him.

This foundation should permeate the entire church in whatever we do. Every time we make a decision, analyze a problem, or meet a challenge, we need to seek His Word. The Bible needs to be our text book, our manual for living, our seminar for Church growth, our book of discipline, and our plan of action.

This requires a different thought process. Instead of determining "what is reasonable" or "what the majority want," or, "what they do", we must seek all the information we can find in God's Word and, through prayer, seek His Divine Will. It requires total submission to His Word. This is the foundation for His Church.

THE MEMBERS

We become part of Christ's Body when we hear, believe, repent, confess, and are baptized for the taking away of our sins. He makes us part of His body, giving us the Holy Spirit. When He does this, we are a part of His Church. We have to sign no doctrinal statements; we have to submit to no approvals by any earthly person.

If this is true, what do we do about the local membership? We need to know who is a member and who is not a member. Many times there are votes to be taken and decisions to be made for the local church. We need to know who are local church members so we can effectively make these decisions. We have a hint in the book of Acts, where Paul is introduced to the Jerusalem church. Barnabus did the job, introducing Paul to them and allaying their fears because of Paul's past of seeking out Christians and killing them. Paul had changed and Barnabus was a witness to that change. Ananias had undoubtedly done a similar thing when he introduced Paul to the church at Damascus.

Let us try to implement a similar plan for the church today. Assume the Johnsons are moving from the Portland Church to the Seattle Church. There, they are greeted by the Smiths. The Smiths get to know the Johnsons, helping them get acquainted with the Seattle Church. When the time comes for the Johnsons to transfer their local membership, the Smiths could introduce them to the Seattle Church, telling the Church a little about these new-found brothers and sisters.

On the other hand, we need to look closely at what the scriptures say about membership. Don, a great Christian man, attended the church where I was an elder. After Don had attended for a while, I went to him and asked him why he had not placed fellowship with the local church. He replied, "I attend here regularly; I give here regularly; I am actively involved. What more do you want?" I thought about this for a while, and then I decided that, according to the Word, he was right. He was already a member of Christ's Church. From that day on I considered him a member of the local church, too. We need to be careful about requiring any more than Christ required as a condition for membership. My opinion is that transfer of membership can be declared by doing it publicly or by simply mentioning it to one of the elders.

What does membership infer? It implies that we have the Holy Spirit in us as with all other members. This means that the leadership needs to make members an active part of decision making within the congregation. Many leaders find this difficult to do, preferring to shoulder all the decisions themselves. This is counter to the advice given Moses by Jethro when Jethro discovered that Moses was overworking himself. Jethro told Moses to share the leadership and Moses took his advice. Our elders need to share the leadership of His Church, too.

ORGANIZING HIS CHURCH

How do we organize His Church? The best way is to use His Plan. Note that, in His Plan, His Church bears His Name. After all, the Bride should carry the name of the Bridegroom. If we are starting a new congregation, the first step is to find a person who is committed to building His Church as an evangelist. Once this has been done, a "mother church" should commit to supporting this evangelist to permit the new work to get off the ground. The evangelist should then go about winning souls and help these new converts win more souls. He does this by using God's plan for everything he does. This group will form the seed of the new work. Once the new work is up and going, the evangelist needs to appoint qualified elders and turn the leadership over to them. This is His Plan. Note that the work of an evangelist is not done until he appoints elders.

One church I am familiar with started out using this plan. For twelve years, the evangelist struggled to build up a congregation, until it became quite strong in spirit and in number. However it was not *"set in order"*, (TITUS 1:5) because elders had not been appointed. The evangelist then accepted a call to another church, resigning his position. Because of this, the informal leadership of the congregation was forced to call another evangelist to serve in his place. Within six months, this congregation had closed its doors. The new preacher had brought some significant problems to the church and was not the right man for this ministry. Because there were no elders to whom he reported, there were no elders to deal effectively with him when the problems became apparent. I learned two great lessons from this experience: (1) the evangelist should NEVER leave a work until he has appointed elders, and (2) God knew what He was doing when he ordained that elders should lead the local church. Don't short-change His Plan!

How should existing congregations be organized? Elders should oversee the entire church. This means that they should be freed from doing ministries and permitted to oversee these ministries. Many elders interpret "overseeing" as "overdoing"; that is, they must do it for it to be done right. On the contrary, "overdoing" results in a lack of overseeing. Elders need to concentrate on overseeing, and assign others to tasks so they can effectively oversee without becoming burned out. The business sector recognizes this. It assigns each person to a supervisor whose primary function is to supervise. Supervision is a job in itself.

Notice that the examples we have in the New Testament involve team effort. Christ sent them out two by two; Paul traveled with Barnabus, and then with Silas. There were twelve apostles chosen. Multiple elders are appointed in a local church. Ambassadors were sent with Paul from the Jerusalem Church to deliver their letter to the Antioch Church. Do you get the point? Christ is suggesting we accomplish things with teams. The Bible encourages this, *"Two are better than one because they have a good return for their labor. ... A cord of three strands is not quickly torn apart."* ECCL. 4:9, 12. Thus, we have both example and command to encourage us to use the team approach.

We can implement this in the local church by assigning responsibilities to teams of persons, rather than individuals. Let the individuals within the team make the specific assignments and let them make the decisions for the team (with elder oversight).   For example, there could be a Christian Education Team.   These could make the assignments and the decisions about Christian Education within the Church.   An elder could be a member of this team (but not the chairman) so that oversight could take place.   I have seen this system work well in one church we attended.   Every decision possible was made by the individual teams, rather than imposed upon them by the elders. There were times when the decision was one that should be considered by the elders.   In those cases the elder would simply say, "Please permit me to take this to the elders to get their reading."   There was never an objection or a complaint to doing it this way.   Every such problem was brought to the collective elders who either made the decision or referred it back to the team.

I have always made the assumption that an elder, individually, has no authority beyond any member of His Church.   Only the collective eldership has the right to make decisions.   My reasoning is twofold.   First, there was a reason Christ wanted a team of elders, and only within that team can the collective wisdom of the elders be realized.   Second, there are numerous examples in the New Testament of workers acting as teams.   We need to follow these examples.

It is interesting to note that, in business, research has shown that (a) teams, rather than a hierarchical structure, produce the best results, and (b) decision making at the lowest level provides the best results.   This is exactly what the Bible has been preaching to His Church.   Let's do it!

Deacons can be selected to assist the elders in their efforts.   We think traditionally of deacons as caring for the physical side of the church.   However, we could easily appoint deacons to such tasks as teaching, pastoring, counseling, music, and other "spiritual" ministries.   Let us not limit ourselves because of tradition.

The minister should report directly to the elders. His scope should be clearly defined, for the benefit of both him and the congregation. He should not be a "super-elder" or a bishop. He could be a minister of preaching, or a minister of preaching and evangelism. I suggest the church stay away from calling him a pastor or making him a minister of pastoring. In this manner, the congregation can learn to expect the elders to perform their pastoring role.

SETTING GOALS

Each church needs to set goals for themselves. Quite often, the elders feel that they must set these goals. Imposing goals by a leadership group is usually unsuccessful. It needs to be an approach that seeks suggestions for goals from all members and all teams.

Each team should start with the Bible. What does it say about their mission, both general and specific? Give ardent prayer to these questions. Once this has been done, each team should submit these to the elders. A team can then collate these goals, seeking to find common ground for the church, and suggest these goals to the Church. The Church should then have the opportunity to modify these goals in a spirit of seeking the working of the Holy Spirit in all members. Once this has been done, the goals should be implemented.

One method I have seen used is the SWOT model. In this model, the church analyzes their strengths, weaknesses, opportunities, and threats to these opportunities. By looking at these carefully, the church can suggest a path to success.

A second model uses force fields. What force is preventing you from accomplishing your goal? Once you identify that force, you can then find a strategy for meeting that force.

MEETINGS

The Church needs to decide why they meet. In too many cases, I have seen a great deal of ambiguity in this. Do they meet to celebrate the Lord's Supper, or do they meet to entertain guests? In one mega-church we attended, the Lord's Supper was not served during the main service. However, it was announced that whoever wished could attend a meeting after the service in the "chapel" to celebrate the Lord's Supper. Why did the "main service" meet? It appeared to meet to attract visitors, and the church was very successful in doing this. But which meeting was a meeting of His Church?

Churches today have a great deal of concern about being visitor friendly. We should promote attendance and involvement in order to win people to Christ. However, we need to carefully examine why we meet and compare our analysis with reasons His Church met in the New Testament.

The Lord's Supper

It is of paramount importance that the church meet every Lord's Day to celebrate the Lord's Supper, proclaiming His death until He comes again. This should be the primary focus of that meeting. There are several ways that we can direct attention to this most important rite.

Who should serve the emblems? A missionary friend of mine told me that in Guam, the women of the Church serve the emblems. This is because it is considered part of their role within the home and the church. Many American churches would recoil at this — "Women shouldn't be leading the Church." But look more closely. In the home, the head of the household is to be the man and, most times, you will find the woman serving the table. Why shouldn't this occur within the church? This is a great example of how an American cultural tradition has been elevated to an almost doctrinal position.

Have the emblems down front, where everyone can see them. Make them visible. Some churches provide seats up front for the elders, facing the congregation. However, this takes away from the theme, that we are all equally sinners and that we all share in the act of placing Jesus on the cross for our sins. This should be a "whole-church" function.

Provide a devotion time prior to handing out the emblems. This will be more effective if the men of the church perform the devotion. In doing this, they demonstrate that the Holy Spirit is active in all the church, not just the elders, deacons, and minister. Following the devotion time, provide a prayer over the emblems.

Next, hand out the emblems to the congregation first. Many churches serve the elders or the servers first during the Lord's Supper. There are three problems with this. First, it is downright impolite. You never serve yourself before your guests. Second, the church does not have two classes of members. We are all covered by the same blood, and this service is meant to give that message. Third, can you imagine Jesus turning to the disciples when He washed their feet and saying, "I wish to teach you humility. Therefore, I'll wash my feet first and then I will wash your feet." Can you imagine Him saying at the last supper, "Here is My Body, given for you. Let me first serve myself and then I will serve you." His example was always to serve others first. We need to follow our Master and emulate Him in serving others first.

Distribute the emblems to the congregation. I have seen three different methods used, all of which are effective. In the simultaneous method, each emblem is handed to each member, and they hold onto the emblems. When all have been served the emblems, the entire church then partakes at once. For a large congregation, if there is considerable time involved in the distribution, children make it very difficult for adults to hang onto liquids within a glass without spilling them. Thus, this method works better for small congregations.

For larger congregations, the serial method works best. In this method, as soon as the member is handed the emblem, he/she partakes. I have seen two methods for the serial method. In the first method, the servers serve all members the bread first, and then return to the table, and pick up the fruit of the vine trays and then serve all of the congregation again. In the second method, each server takes two trays, a bread tray and a fruit of the vine tray. The server then passes the bread tray down a row, and follows it with a fruit of the vine tray.

Some churches provide music during the serving of the emblems. If this is done, it should be kept very low volume so that people can pray by themselves during the serving of the emblems.

The Lord's Supper should be central to the entire service. This means that all distractions should be set aside. Announcements can be handled in written form, permitting the meeting to concentrate on more important things.

Offerings

Many churches present the offering after the Lord's Supper. In so doing, they are equating the offering part of the service with the Lord's Supper part of the service. This is exactly what we want to avoid. The Lord's Supper is the reason we are here, not the offering.

In addition, they are, in effect, giving the message, "OK. You've been served some food. Now pony up some cash." This gives entirely the wrong message to both members and visitors. This unwanted message can easily be prevented by eliminating offerings from the service. Use the same method that was used by Paul in the New Testament and Jehoash in the Old Testament — place a box in the hall to receive tithes and offerings from those of a willing heart.

Music

Music can add to the service. However, we need to recognize that the purpose of the music is to elicit active participation by the members. First, the speaker system should be set at a volume that permits people to hear themselves and the people next to them. This gives them the "congregation" feel. Next, songs should be selected so that most of them are known by the people. This gives them "familiarity," feeling a part of the process. Third, songs should be selected that are easy to follow. There are some songs that sound great when sung by a professional, but are hard to sing as a congregation.

My wife and I attended one church that had a terrific team of singers and players on stage. However, the congregation knew none of the songs, and the songs were so complex that they would have been very difficult for the congregation to learn. Thus, there was very little participation from the audience. When we left the service, I turned to Myrna and said, "that was a very nice performance." We need to minimize performance and maximize participation of the church.

BAPTISMS

One of the most important events in the life of His Church is when someone is being born into Christ through baptism. The entire Church should rejoice at this event. The Bible tells us, *"I tell you, there is joy in the presence of the angels of God over one sinner who repents."* LUKE 15:10. If the angels are rejoicing, and they do not have the hope that we have, how much more we should rejoice when someone comes to Him?

Although baptism should take place as soon as a decision has been made for Christ, we should all try to make it to the baptism to witness this great event. In addition we should treat it as something special.   Having a special song or a scripture reading can make it more meaningful.

SUMMARY

We can and should build Christ's Church, today.   In it we can find the happiness in serving Him and growing in Him. In it we can find the comfort in hard times and the joy of sharing in good times.   In it we can find the wisdom of elders and the enthusiasm of youth.   In His Church, we can find Christ Himself and enjoy being the kind of person that God created us to be.

Chapter 13

WHAT CAN I DO AS AN INDIVIDUAL?

INTRODUCTION

This is a very important question. The Bible is a book of action — impelling us to do, and not just to think or say. In this chapter, we shall look at some specific actions we can take to draw us closer to His Church.

BECOME HIS

The first, and most important thing you should do is to obey Christ's plan of salvation and become one of His. Each of us needs to hear, believe, repent, confess, be baptized for remission of sins, and live a holy life. Although I had been baptized when I was in high school, years later I decided that I was unsure of the reason for that baptism. Was it for remission of sins or was it because I had already "taken Jesus into my heart?" [A reason not in conformity with His Word]. Since I was unsure, I was rebaptized for the remission of my sins. Be sure you follow His Plan of Salvation, too. Make it right in your life.

Becoming His carries, with it, many concurrent beliefs. Since Jesus is our Lord, everything we do and everything we own is His. Our goals for our lives are predicated on what He wants for us. Our possessions are His and are to be used for His benefit. Our time is His and our energies are His. We belong totally to Him. This is a lifelong commitment and we should take it very seriously.

STUDY HIS WORD

The second thing you can do is to study His Word. How are you to know His will for your life if you do not read what He has said to you? This would be like marrying and never communicating with your spouse. It would make no sense at all. Therefore, get to know Him through His word.

The Bible has a total of 1189 chapters. By reading 3.26 chapters per day, a person can read through the entire Bible in one year. Make it a practice to read at least four chapters per day. Not only read His word, but study His word. Think about what you've read and how you can apply it to your life. Pray about what you've read. Really study the passage. *"Be diligent to present yourself approved to God as a workman who does not need to be ashamed, handling accurately the word of truth."* 2 TIM. 2:15. Handling accurately is done through study. An early writer speaks of the result, *"When you have read and carefully listened to these things, you shall know what God bestows on such as rightly love Him, being made [as ye are] a paradise of delight, presenting in yourselves a tree bearing all kinds of produce and flourishing well, being adorned with various fruits."* [133]

USE BIBLICAL TERMS

Use the vocabulary that Christ uses in His Word. For starters, give credit to Christ for His Church. Don't use the terms, "my church" or "our church". Use the term, pastor, correctly: apply it to the elders. Call the preacher a minister or a preacher: don't call him a reverend or a pastor. Refer to the building as "the church building" and not "the church." In other words, apply Biblical terms to your daily life. Make the Bible real in your vocabulary. A pure vocabulary can lead to clear thinking about His Word. The Scripture says, *"For the mouth speaks out of that which fills the heart."* MATT. 12:34. If we are

---

[133] *Epistle of Mathetes to Diognetus*, Ch. 12

to think clearly about the Bible, we have to adopt a vocabulary that is clearly Biblical. Clement of Rome (95 AD) places use of words among the Christian virtues to which we should strive, *"Let a man be faithful: let him be powerful in the utterance of knowledge; let him be wise in judging of words; let him be pure in all his deeds; yet the more he seems to be superior to others [in these respects], the more humble-minded ought he to be, and to seek the common good of all, and not merely his own advantage."* [134]

BE YE SEPARATE

Live a life that is in the world but separate from the world. These early Christians did just that. Life around them was similar to life today. There was immodesty all around them. Ignatius (106 AD) writes, *"And why dost thou abuse the nature of the Virgin, and style her members disgraceful, since thou didst of old display such in public processions, and didst order them to be exhibited naked, males in the sight of females, and females to stir up the unbridled lust of males? But now these are reckoned by thee disgraceful, and thou pretendest to be full of modesty, thou spirit of fornication, not knowing that then only anything becomes disgraceful when it is polluted by wickedness."* [135] Public baths were a place of immodesty. Clement of Alexandria (200 AD) writes, *"They will scarce strip before their own husbands affecting a plausible pretence of modesty; but any others who wish, may see them at home shut up naked in their baths. ... as if their modesty had been washed away in the bath."* [136] We need to make sure that our modesty, too, is not being washed off by the society of our day. As the Bible says, *"Likewise, I want women to adorn themselves with proper clothing, modestly and discreetly, not*

---

[134] Clement, *Epistle to the Corinthians,* Ch. 48
[135] Ignatius, *Epistle to the Philippians,* Ch. 6
[136] Clement of Alexander, *The Instructor,* Book 3, Ch. 5

with braided hair and gold or pearls or costly garments; but rather by means of good works, as befits women making a claim to godliness." 1 TIM. 2:9.

There were "games" in arenas at which horrible things were done: animals were set on animals, people were set upon by wild animals, people were to fight to the death with other people. All this was in the name of entertainment. They couldn't get enough blood and gore. In theaters, also, actors performed sexually explicit acts, all in the name of entertainment. Mucius Felix (198 AD) writes, *"For in the chariot games who does not shudder at the madness of the people brawling among themselves? or at the teaching of murder in the gladiatorial games? In the scenic games also the madness is not less, but the debauchery is more prolonged: for now a mimic either expounds or shows forth adulteries; now nerveless player, while he feigns lust, suggests it; the same actor disgraces your gods by attributing to them adulteries, sighs, hatreds; the same provokes your tears with pretended sufferings, with vain gestures and expressions. Thus you demand murder, in fact, while you weep at it in fiction."* [137]

We see this same decadent philosophy today in our television, movies, and video games. Our society, too, cannot get enough gore. We, as Christians, need to give our attention to the "things above." Paul says, *"Finally, brethren, whatever is true, whatever is honorable, whatever is right, whatever is pure, whatever is lovely, whatever is of good repute, if there is any excellence and if anything worthy of praise, let your mind dwell on these things."* PHIL. 4:8. We need to do precisely this — to focus on the uplifting. God has given each of us free will. We need to will to be free by choosing Godly things, rather than the world's things.

---

[137] *The Octavius of Minucius Felix,* Ch. 37

BE DEDICATED IN MARRIAGE

We need to be dedicated in our marriages. When we marry, it should be for life. When we run into trouble, we should not be afraid to seek help. A few years ago, after being married for 25 years, my wife and I ran into an issue that we could not resolve among ourselves. It had to do with the priority the church should have in our lives. We both sat down and agreed to seek the counsel of the preacher who married us. By this time, he and his wife were in their 80's, so we knew they had the wisdom and experience to advise us in accordance with Christ. To make a long story short, he set me straight in about five minutes. I was wrong and, when I heard it from this dear elder servant, I knew it. I tell you this true story to illustrate that you are never too old to seek wise counsel from someone older than you. God wants us to have good marriages, so let us work diligently to have good marriages — for ourselves and for our Master.

WITNESS TO OTHERS

Christ has asked us to witness to others. *"Go therefore and make disciples of all the nations, baptizing them in the name of the Father and the Son and the Holy Spirit,"* MATT. 28:18. Some Christians find this difficult to do. However, let me give you some suggestions.

My wife and I were traveling to our home and found ourselves in Idaho Falls, Idaho one Sunday morning. Therefore, we stopped in and worshipped with a local church. The minister, a plain, unassuming man with a soft voice, preached a great, simple sermon on witnessing. He used the text of John 4:7-42, where Jesus spoke to the Samaritan woman. His final point was, "How do I begin to witness?" His answer was, "Offer them a drink of water. That's what Jesus did." That is witnessing in its purest form. Offer someone a drink of water and, then, tell them how you depend upon Jesus in your life. That's it. No great theological discussion, just one person telling another about their God.

As discussions develop, there are several methods or programs that one can use to teach people of Christ. One I've used is to open the book of Acts and have people outline what these people did to be saved. This works very well with people who have some knowledge of Christ, but have little knowledge of God's Plan for Salvation.

For those who have little knowledge of the Bible, we have used the five video tapes from the Jule Miller, "Visual Bible Study Series" with great success. These are available from Gospel Services, Inc., Houston, Texas. The series has five tapes that cover the whole Bible: "The Patriarchal Age", "The Mosaic Age", "The Christian Age", "God's Plan for Redeeming Man", and "History of the Lord's Church". They also come with workbooks. My wife and I purchased these tapes and keep them handy. We have also loaned them out numerous times to others who are teaching their friends about Christ.

Once someone commits to Christ, they need to have their sins remitted through baptism. You taught them — you baptize them. This will be one of the greatest events in your life, so enjoy it. When divisions occurred in the Corinthian Church, Paul said, *"I thank God that I baptized none of you except Crispus and Gaius, that no man should say you were baptized in my name."* 1 COR. 1:14. Who do you think did the baptizing, if Paul didn't? The people of the church. Who baptized the 3000 on the day of Pentecost? The people of the church. So, you do it, too.

BECOME ACTIVE IN HIS CHURCH

In addition to this, each of us needs to become active in His Church. God created us as social beings and we need this social and spiritual contact. A number of years ago, Myrna and I moved to Las Vegas, where I was employed at the Nevada Test Site. All around us in Las Vegas we saw gambling, sex, and practically every evil one could imagine: there was a Go-Go club in the high school, to teach young ladies how to be Go-Go dancers; the high school students played craps during lunch hours. We became involved with Christ's Church, there, and found ourselves spending many evenings at the church building or with church friends. The Church became the center of our social life — and it was a very strong church because all of us recognized the importance it had in our lives. The Church grew by leaps and bounds, and we grew spiritually by leaps and bounds. God was working in the lives of many there. I remember one lady who owned a tavern; she decided to get out of the business when she came to Christ.

Today, we need the church as much or more. All around us are things, people, and environments that are trying to distract us from being the kind of priests that Christ wants us to be. In His Church, we can find encouragement from others to live the pure life He wants for us.

There is a second reason we should attend regularly. We are told, *"And He gave some as apostles, and some as prophets, and some as evangelists, and some as pastors and teachers, for the equipping of the saints for the work of service, to the building up of the body of Christ;"* EPH. 4:11-12. I have previously used this passage to analyze the offices within the church. Now look at this passage from the members' point of view. What is it we are supposed to do? We are to build up the body. We cannot do this task without meeting with the body. If we are not there, someone is not being built up. We need to fulfill this mission God has given each of us — to build up His body.

Finally, we need to permit the Holy Spirit to speak through us in causing the Church to grow into His Church. Where there are problems, or where the church has departed from His Plan, we need to lovingly make this known and be an agent of change to bring the church back into conformity with

His Word. The Holy Spirit can and does work through each of us working His will. We should not quench this Spirit, but give Him voice and permit His Church to grow more into His image.

LOVE THE BRETHREN

Americans are very competitive. For this reason, we sometimes shy away from those who do not believe precisely as we do. We want to win others to "our side." However, in Christ's Church, He is "our side," and Satan is "their side." Between Christians, there should only be love — not competition.

One of the great examples of this is the love between Polycarp and Ignatius (106, 110 AD). Polycarp obviously believed that the church was to be led by a plurality of elders, whereas Ignatius believed that the church should have a bishop, with elders reporting to him. But examine how revered Ignatius is to Polycarp, *"I exhort you all, therefore, to yield obedience to the word of righteousness, and to exercise all patience, such as ye have seen [set] before your eyes, not only in the case of the blessed Ignatius, and Zosimus, and Rufus, but also in others among yourselves, and in Paul himself, and the rest of the apostles."* [138] He calls Ignatius righteous, patient, and blessed — in spite of the differences between them. This is exemplary love — the love we need to emulate. In like manner, Ignatius referred to Polycarp as *"most blessed in God"*, *"blameless face,"* and *"clothed in grace."* [139] These martyrs had a knack for seeing God in others and responding to the indwelling of the Holy Spirit in all Christians. We, too, need to hone this skill, to love those whom the Father loves.

But how do we do this? How can we develop a close relationship with someone who does not believe precisely as we

---

[138] Polycarp, *Epistle to the Philippians*, Ch. 9
[139] Ignatius, *Epistle to Polycarp*, Ch. 1 and Ch. 7

do? The answer lies in accepting the Fatherhood of God. We are all in the same class — the class of sinners — and we all have the same Father. Because I am not your father, I can accept you as you are — a sinner like me. Neither you nor I have attained to that perfection that Christ desires. Because of this, I do not consider myself worthy of keeping track of your sins; I must concentrate on keeping track of my sins, and improving my relationship with my Father day by day.

I recently attended a marriage of a great Christian man to a great Christian woman. Both had been divorced. As I expressed above, my feeble knowledge of the Bible tells me that for me to marry a divorcee would be committing a sin — the sin of adultery. However, I know that I am fallible. I do not have perfect knowledge, nor do I practice perfect Christianity. I believe that I have no right to judge whether someone else commits a sin or is in sin; only the Father has this right. My right and my obligation in life is to love those whom God loves and to share my feeble knowledge of God with them. It is up to them to consider my words, to examine God's word, and to put into practice that which His word teaches. I know that God loves this couple and I see God in their lives every day that they live. I see them daily performing acts of love, studying the Word, and practicing the love that Christ teaches. In fact, I have been the recipient of their love. I can easily accept them as a Godly couple, because I believe in them, that they are daily working to improve their relationship with our shared Father. I not only accept them, I genuinely love them and wish their marriage the greatest of success, because I know that they are building their marriage on Christ and His Word.

"But," you say, "You are compromising your beliefs." On the contrary. I still have the beliefs I have. However, I recognize that I am a sinner. I am imperfect – and that imperfection extends to my understanding of God and how to apply His Word. Therefore, my obligation is to obey God to the best of my ability, to share the feeble knowledge I have of God with others, and to love those precious persons who are obeying God to the best of their ability. It is not my job to usurp the Father by acting as the parent in this relationship, when I am, in fact, only a brother.

We need to strive diligently to be humble in spirit, bold in God's Word, and, above all, to love the brethren with a love that goes past our own beliefs and understandings and strives to emulate the depth of God's love for us. We need to genuinely love those who love God — to appreciate their love for God and relish in the sharing we have through the Father's love and Christ's sacrifice. In this world of sin, violence, and unkindness, these God-lovers shine as a beacon to fill our lives with the light of Christ and His Love. How they enrich our lives!!

SUMMARY

We need not let the world mold us into its shape. *"And do not be conformed to this world, but be transformed by the renewing of your mind, that you may prove what the will of God is, that which is good and acceptable and perfect."* ROM. 12:2. We can and should become a vital part of His Church: (1) one who grows in Him day by day through study and prayer, (2) one who is in the world, but is not of the world, (3) one who actively participates in His Church and, (4) most of all, one who loves unselfishly and completely. It is only in these acts that we can transform "our church" into "His Church" in our lives. In so doing, we can and will become a homing signal to those around us, guiding others to the Great Physician. Others will come to see that we are different — we are holy as He is holy. They will be able to see Him in everything we say and do.

AN INVITATION

If you have not had your sins washed away by Christ, now is the time. His Plan requires that you (a) Hear His message, (b) Believe that He is the Son of God, (c) Repent of your sins, (d) Confess Him as Christ and Lord in your life, and (e) Be immersed in Christian baptism for the remission of your sins. If you have not done this, you have not obeyed the Lord; you have not followed His Plan. It is not our plan that determines salvation, but His Plan. Read about the nine conversions in Acts and, from them, learn what you must do to be saved.

Finally, do it! Become a part of His Body and know the blessing of having the Holy Spirit guiding your life. It will mean happiness in this life and joy for eternity.